Please return / renew by date shown.
You can renew at:
norlink.norfolk.gov.uk
or by telephone: 0844 800 8006
Please have your library card & PIN ready.

NORTH WALSHAM LIBRARY

Tel. 01692 402182

03. FEB 06.

04. MAY 06.

30. OCT 06.

03.10.08

(Front Cover) An early Saxon village in the 6th century. In the foreground a building-timber being dressed with an axe. Beyond, a pole-lathe, for the production of wooden vessels, lies idle.

Norfolk Origins

4:THE NORTH FOLK;
ANGLES, SAXONS & DANES

Richard Bond, Kenneth Penn
and Andrew Rogerson
in collaboration with the Norfolk Museums Service

Illustrations: Susan White
Photographs: Norfolk Archaeological Unit

Other titles in the Norfolk Origins series:
1: Hunters to First Farmers (published 1981)
2: Roads and Tracks (published 1983)
3: Celtic Fire and Roman Rule (published 1987)

Text © Richard Bond, Kenneth Penn and Andrew Rogerson
Drawings © Sue White 1990
ISBN:0 946148 43 0
Published by Poppyland Publishing, North Walsham, Norfolk 1990
Designed by Top Floor Design, Norwich
Printed by Printing Services (Norwich) Ltd
Typeset by PTPS, Norwich
Printed in Great Britain

Warning
Reference to or representation of a site, track or road should not be taken as evidence that
such a site, track or road can be seen or may be visited. In many cases sites are on private
land.

Contents

Introduction

The Anglo-Saxon period was immensely long, spanning some 600 years from the end of the Roman period, traditionally set at 410 AD (although historians debate this period endlessly), to the Norman Conquest in 1066.

To the women who sat sewing the Bayeux Tapestry, that remarkable picture-story of the defeat of Harold by Duke William, those early centuries must have seemed impossibly remote. To us they remain a Dark Age within which we struggle to make sense of myth and legend, endeavouring to find facts in ancient remains and garbled stories.

Norfolk – part of the kingdom of the East Angles – saw many changes in those six centuries; here we attempt to describe and explain them.

Devil's Dyke. Swaffham-Downham Market Road, looking south April 1990 (Copyright Poppyland Photos)

SETTING THE SCENE

The Landscape

The ancient kingdom of the East Angles – Norfolk, Suffolk and parts of Cambridgeshire – was a low country, its surface smoothed by ice sheets which left great areas of sands, gravels and clays as they thawed. Cromer Ridge, rising to 300 feet, is the largest of the few hilly features left by the ice.

Before the 18th century large tracts of Norfolk (mostly the sandy and gravelly areas) were still virtual deserts of poor, uninhabited heathland used only for grazing, despaired of by agricultural reformers. Mousehold Heath is a relic of a vast sprawling heath which stretched miles to the east and north. Remnants of this forbidding landscape can still be glimpsed around Sandringham and in sandy Breckland near Thetford. Wretham Heath is a fine example.

Much of the remaining common heaths was enclosed in the late 18th and early 19th centuries, creating large rectangular fields, best seen today in the Swaffham, Thetford and Bury St Edmunds areas.

In the Anglo-Saxon period the few villages in these places were mainly in stream valleys or beside meres. The -ford names of Lynford, Ickford, Thetford and Mundford show they were close to streams. Villages were surrounded by little more than patches of cultivated land. Heathland yielded only slowly to the plough.

It is likely that within a century of the coming of the Anglo-Saxons, their settlements had been established in every part of "upland" Norfolk, not only on the light but also on the heavier soils. These farms and villages lay close to former Roman settlements but rarely over them.

In areas of medium and heavy soils many villages were first established as outlying woodland or pastoral settlements, away from the main centres. Examples include Holt (meaning wood), Rockland (rook wood), Gateley (goat clearing), Edgefield (meadow field) and Keswick (cheese farm).

The large belt of woodland on the boulder clays of central Norfolk and Suffolk recorded in the Domesday Book was probably a mixture of wood pasture (seasonal grazing) and coppiced woods, valued by the Anglo-Saxons as a source of building timber.

The great alluvial basin of the Fens, rimmed to the east and south by a low ridge of chalk, formed a natural frontier for the early Saxon kingdom of the East Angles. The Romans had drained, settled and farmed parts of the Fens, but after the collapse of their authority the area reverted to a wet wilderness.

Settlements were limited to low islands, such as Southery, and to the band of higher silts at the mouth of the basin, stretching from West Lynn to

Wisbech and beyond. Even by the end of the Saxon period, when much of the Fens had been made into rich grazing land, the major Domesday Book settlements were strung out in a line along the higher silts around the southern edge of the Wash, including Terrington St Clement and Walpole St Andrew.

In Roman times East Norfolk was dominated by a great estuary which flowed through the valleys of the Yare, Wensum, Waveney, Bure and Ant. It entered the sea between the forts of Caister and Burgh Castle and extended behind the islands of Flegg and Lothing.

Norwich, the first good landfall on the Wensum, was at the very head of the estuary where an east-west Roman road crossed the river at Bishop's Bridge. The town was well established by 900 as one of the great ports of the kingdom and it traded with the continent.

Yarmouth and Lynn were established much later. Yarmouth, situated on a sand spit at the mouth of the estuary, became a trading port in the 11th century. Lynn, at the mouth of the river Nar, was founded at the end of the same century by Herbert de Losinga, Bishop of Norwich.

Thetford emerged as a port at the confluence of the Little Ouse and Thet after the Danes, in 869, built a camp where a major land route, the Icknield Way, entered Norfolk across an important ford, Thet-ford (meaning people's ford).

The Saxon population was scattered and sparse, although it grew remarkably through the period. Peasants were isolated on farms and estates and only the horse-borne nobility could travel far. Some Roman roads, including Peddars Way, Pye Road (the present A140) and Stone Road (the A144), remained in use. Otherwise little is known of the Saxon road system.

By the time of the Norman Conquest, England was long-settled and with a complicated array of institutions and systems of landholding. The Domesday Book bears testimony to its wealth and complexity. A church stood in nearly every village and land was minutely parcelled out and intensively cultivated. The large estates which had been the norm in early Saxon times had been broken up into smaller holdings, the typical Norfolk peasant farmer having perhaps as little as 30 acres.

North Sea Raiders and the Saxon Shore

For nearly four centuries the Roman province of Britannia was part of a huge, civilised empire. Yet within a few turbulent years it slipped away from imperial control, virtually abandoned to its own defence by Emperor Honorius in 410.

In these centuries the empire had changed greatly; massive inflation, social unrest and threats from beyond the frontiers had shaken its foundations.

Troubles mounted in the 3rd century when ever-threatening Germanic tribes, under pressure from other nomadic tribes in the east, took to the sea and raided the coasts of Gaul and Britannia. Their surprise attacks met little resistance from the Roman army which, though powerful, was usually distant. Its only response was to build a series of coastal forts for a new naval and land patrol force under the single command of a general, the Count of the Saxon Shore (Comes Litoris Saxonici).

The British forts ran from Portchester, near Portsmouth, in the south, to Brancaster (Branodunum) on the North Norfolk coast. Two forts, one of which was possibly called Garionnonum, were built facing each other, at Burgh Castle and Caister-on-Sea at the mouth of the estuary. The Romans called this coast the Saxon Shore (Litus Saxonicum), and the forts represented a move to an increasingly defensive position against the Anglo-Saxon raiders.

In 367 Britain suffered a series of attacks, dubbed the Barbarian Conspiracy by Roman authors, which resulted in widespread destruction. Large areas were plundered by Saxons and Franks from the continent, Picts from Scotland, Scots from Ireland, and the Attacotti, who were probably based in the western isles.

The Count of the Saxon Shore, Nectaridus, was killed, and Fullofaudes, the chief commander of Roman land forces, captured. Not until 369 did Theodosius, a general sent by the Emperor Valentinian, restore some order to the province.

A Province Abandoned

As we have seen, the traditional date for the abandonment of Britain by the Romans is 410. A century later, much of eastern England was in Anglo-Saxon hands and the indigenous British appear to have vanished. How this happened is unclear and the stuff of legend.

In 401 the barbarian leader Alaric the Visigoth led his men into Italy in a long campaign which ended in the submission of Rome in 410. In Britain a succession of usurpers, including Marcus, Gratian and Constantine III, challenged the Roman emperor. On the continent the Vandals, a Germanic tribe, crossed the Rhine and seized Gaul, which was to become a stepping stone for raids on the British coast.

According to the Greek historian Zosimus, a British revolt in about 409 expelled Roman officials, freed cities from barbarians – possibly barbarian troops – and overturned Roman laws. From then on Britain remained under the control of "local tyrants". One of these was called Proud Tyrant (Superbus Tyrannus) by the 6th century British moralist Gildas. The Anglo-Saxon historian Bede (circa 680-735) called him Vortigern.

Despite opposition, Vortigern settled Germanic mercenaries somewhere in England in about 430 (whose leaders are known to us as Hengist and Horsa) to guard against Picts, Scots and even possible intervention by Roman troops sent from Gaul to recover Britain.

Although no longer part of the empire, Britain was in many ways still a Roman island after 410 with a native ruler relying on foreign troops for support. Such a reliance was fatal, involving a Christian ruler isolated from his fellow Britons in the hands of pagan foreigners.

The Great Migration

Vortigern's settlement of his Anglo-Saxon "allies" opened the way for a large influx of migrants.

Lured by the promise of riches and fertile land, the settlers made the hazardous voyage across the sea, sure of a safe reception in areas controlled by mercenaries. The trip required enormous resources and organisation, not least to build and equip boats for up to 60 people which were rowed across the open sea.

Copied from a 4th century Roman drawing, this boat is of the type that carried the Germanic settlers over the North Sea to our shores.

Behind their war leaders the Angles and Saxons – men, women and children – arrived in such huge numbers that the Anglian homeland of South Denmark was almost completely deserted. So many came that a violent takeover became inevitable.

Writing in the 6th century, Gildas the British churchman, says: "All the major towns were laid low by the repeated battering of enemy rams; laid low, too, (were) all the inhabitants – church leaders, priests and people alike, as the swords glinted all around and the flames crackled.It was a sad sight. In the middle of the squares the foundation stones of high walls and towers that had been torn from their lofty base, holy altars, fragments of corpses, covered with a purple crust of congealed blood, looked as though they had been mixed up in some dreadful wine-press. There was no burial to be had except in the ruins of houses or the bellies of beasts and birds."

Historians have been unwilling to accept this lurid account and yet, when the Anglo-Saxons became literate and wrote their dynastic histories, they too remembered their conquest as having been accompanied by battles and bloodshed.

The early Germanic and Scandinavian invaders were mixed and included Angles, Saxons, Frisians and Jutes. But by circa 500, two generations later, the Anglo-Saxon areas of Norfolk and Suffolk were to some extent distinct from the East Saxons across the Stour. This suggests a unity of sorts among the new East Angles.

Although we do not know how many Germanic settlers arrived during the migration period, nor how many of the indigenous British survived in the upheavals of the invasion, there is no doubt that the population in, say, 500 was a small fraction of what it had been in the 4th century. Early Saxon England was almost empty of inhabitants when compared with its densely settled late Roman predecessor.

Whilst the indigenous British continued in the west of England, in the east they appear to have been absorbed into the culture and pagan religion of the newcomers. Their Celtic language disappeared and was replaced by English, but not before a few place names were adopted by the settlers. Branodunum became Brancaster and the name of the Yare and the two villages called Eccles (from *ecclesia*, Latin for church) survived.

Many people were reduced to serfdom. The Anglo-Saxon word for foreigner and slave, *walh*, was applied to them, giving us names like Walsham and Walcot, and probably Walton, Walpole and Walsoken in the Fens, and of course the modern word Welsh.

In places it is conceivable that an Anglo-Saxon warrior took over an old Roman district and founded a dynasty, perhaps with his headquarters within the walls of a deserted town and with a cemetery for his people nearby. It is likely, for example, that in the 5th century an Anglian chief established himself at Caistor-by-Norwich and that his followers were buried in the great early Saxon cemetery just outside the walls of the old Roman town. Saxon material of the 8th and 9th centuries has also been found nearby.

It may be that the settlers learned to call deserted forts and towns castor or chester (from *castra*, Latin for fort), so that Venta Icenorum became Caistor St Edmund.

We believe that many settlers came to East Anglia early in the 5th century. Although we have no historical evidence, the witness of the Anglo-Saxon cemeteries, and perhaps place names, point to early settlement, that is to migration on a large scale by 450 at the latest.

Angles, Saxons and Frisians

Writing about the Anglo-Saxon invaders, Bede, in a famous passage, says: "These newcomers were from the three most formidable races of Germany, the Saxons, Angles and Jutes ... From the Angles, that is the country known as Angulus, which lies between the provinces of the Jutes and Saxons and is said to remain unpopulated to this day, are descended the East and Middle Angles, the Mercians, all the Northumbrian stock and the other English peoples."

Bede also mentions other small "tribes" which came; some are remembered in place names. People from Friesland, on the Dutch coast, gave their name to Friston and Freston, in Suffolk; the Swabians, from South Germany, gave theirs to Swaffham; the Spalda gave theirs to Spalding (Lincolnshire).

Elsewhere, early tribal names can be discerned from the Norfolk villages of Fring (Frea's people), Hickling (Hicel's people) and Longham (Lawa's people).

The Anglo-Saxons remembered their homelands across the sea and may have brought some village names with them. It may be, for example, that the Low Country names of Dokkum, Gislum, Barrum and Blya became the Norfolk and Suffolk villages of Docking, Gisleham, Barham and Bly.

Written sources

The early Anglo-Saxon period (circa 410-650) is often called the Dark Ages – because it is so dark to us.

As the early Anglo-Saxons were illiterate, written sources are few, provided by distant or foreign writers with no special interest in contemporary Anglo-Saxon life, or by later churchmen who had little wish to record a pagan past.

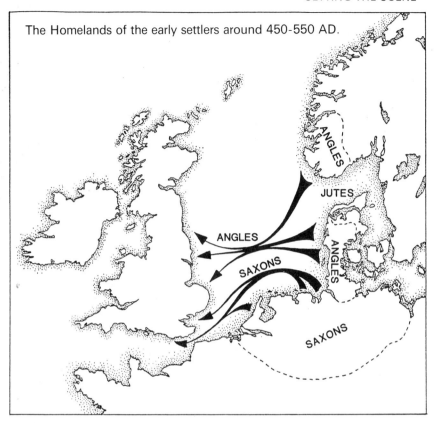

The Homelands of the early settlers around 450-550 AD.

The homelands of the early settlers.

They did have an alphabet, consisting of the runes, but this was not used casually; instead, the runes had a magical significance and were made into spells (hence the word "spelling"). Even the famous poem Beowulf, which draws a powerful picture of early society, is a later Christian work looking back to an imagined world of heroes and dragons.

The earliest work of any length comes from the Celtic west of Britain and was written in about 550 by Gildas, the British churchman who was a contemporary of the first English kings. In his 'Ruin of Britain' he writes about the wicked kings of the Celtic west and their corrupt priests, telling how their vice and neglect incurred the wrath of God in the shape of "impious easterners" – the Anglo-Saxons.

He writes: "Britain has kings, but they are tyrants; she has judges, but they are wicked. They often plunder and terrorise the innocent; they

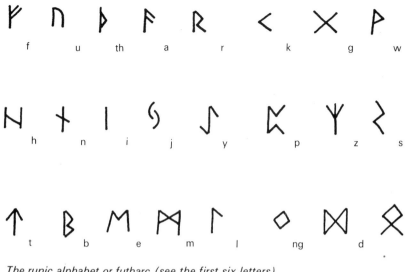

The runic alphabet or futharc (see the first six letters)

defend and protect the guilty and thieving; they have many wives – whores and adulteresses; they constantly swear false oaths; they make vows but almost at once tell lies; they wage wars – civil and unjust."

Bede, the Anglo-Saxon churchman writing in a monastery at Jarrow in about 730 AD, is our greatest source. His 'History of the English Church and People', written for an aristocratic audience, gives examples of how the devotion of Christian Anglo-Saxon kings brought rewards for their peoples.

Bede did not set out to record the old heroes of a pagan past but to draw a clear picture of kings and saints struggling to bring England out of a heathen darkness. Thus the heathen past remains dark to us. His ideal was a single English nation under one Roman church and one king.

One other source is the Anglo-Saxon Chronicle, inspired by King Alfred in about 890 and drawn from Bede, Gildas, legend and early annals. Started by the West Saxons to promote their own cause, it tells us little about East Anglia, a kingdom successively conquered and made subject to Mercians, Danes and West Saxons.

Archaeology

The Roman world shared a Mediterranean culture which was monumental, urban and literate. A complex, ordered society of towns, temples and market squares, it had a remarkable material culture complete with schools, pensions and even burial clubs.

By contrast, the Anglo-Saxons were illiterate country folk who built in wood and thatch and had simple lifestyles. Their unrecorded lives are best understood through their remains.

Several of their excavated settlements near the coasts of Germany, Denmark and the Low Countries reveal quite impressive villages, often of longhouses set in fenced enclosures round a green or along a street. Some

Within an early Saxon 'hut', tablet-weaving, spinning, and the loom will soon be busy.

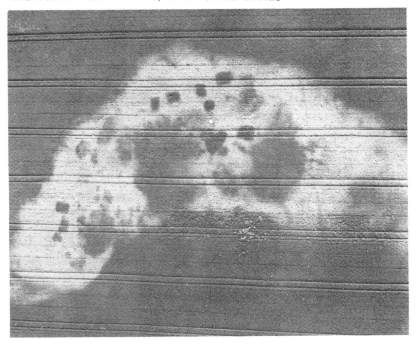

A group of cropmarks shows up clearly in a patch of light soil, near Acle. They may be traces of Early Saxon 'sunken-featured' buildings. (Derek Edwards – Norfolk Archaeological Unit)

settlements in the coastal saltmarshes, built on deliberately raised mounds above the threat of flooding, were also deserted, presumably for a new land across the sea.

Some early English settlements have fenced hallhouses set neatly in groups. Strangely, the longhouse, so common on the continent, is hardly found in England; it is thought that a milder climate and more sheep-raising made them unnecessary.

Of the few East Anglian settlements so far excavated, the best example is at West Stow, near Bury St Edmunds, where a small village on a sandy hillock next to the river Lark has been dug and partly reconstructed. There, one can stand inside a wooden hallhouse and a "sunken" hut where a loom once stood. West Stow was self-sufficient and inhabited throughout the year by several families.

Historians and archaeologists are revealing how villages may have fitted into the social hierarchy and geography of the early kingdoms of

Anglo-Saxon England. This is important in Norfolk where no early charters survive.

Archaeologically, early Anglo-Saxons are more familiar in death than in life. In their cemeteries they buried their dead with "gravegoods" – women with beads and brooches, men with shields, spears and, rarely, swords. Some objects worn by women, such as wristclasps and girdlehangers, are distinctly Anglian, reflecting a difference in dress custom from the women of Saxon Essex. These gravegoods are like those found on the continent, but only in the "Anglian" area of Denmark, Sweden and Norway. Neither is there any hint in these cemeteries of British people; the gravegoods are resolutely Germanic.

By studying bones and cremated fragments in burial urns, specialists are trying to reconstruct the population, age at death and sex of the early Anglo-Saxons. Clues are given by the "richness" of the burial and the variety of gravegoods. From these remains it is possible to guess whether the dead were slaves, freemen or nobility, or even of royal birth, as at Sutton Hoo, Suffolk.

A pair of gorgeously decorated gilt bronze wrist-clasps (ladies' cuff-links) from a grave at Morningthorpe. (David Wicks – Norfolk Archaeological Unit)

A PAGAN PEOPLE AND THEIR SETTLEMENTS

Leaders and peasants

Contrary to popular imagination, the immigrants did not settle as free and equal men in some infant democracy. Anglo-Saxon society was violent and strictly hierarchical, governed by all-powerful noblemen and supported by the forced labour of slaves. The main tribal dynasties were established by 550.

The lord, sometimes raised by ancestry or chosen as a war leader from the tribal aristocracy, was the centre of all – the giver of wealth, land, status and weapons, the source of justice, the governor of tribal religion and the provider of bread. Hlaford, the Anglo-Saxon word for lord, is derived from hlaf-weard, meaning the provider of bread. His retainers shared his hall (his mead hall), his food and drink and were bound in loyalty to him until death.

The tribal leaders, some of whom were kings, led the kindred – or *cynn* – in battle. The word king comes from the Anglo-Saxon word *cynn*, pronounced "kin." In times of war the kings rewarded their followers' loyalty. Indeed, war was often waged for just this purpose – kings robbed their neighbours to placate their own men.

Lords regulated strict tribal customs and laws, under which every crime had a price and every man a value. Any Anglo-Saxon man who committed adultery had to provide the wronged husband with a new wife. A groom who expected a virgin bride but was disappointed could return her to her family and get his money back.

Above all, in a brutal society, the *cynn* (both king and kindred) offered peace, security and protection without which a man was outcast. To be lordless was a shameful fate, a fact which helped bind the *cynn* together. The plight of the outcast was a common theme of poetry recited by Anglo-Saxon minstrels, called scops, in feast halls.

"He knows who makes trial how harsh and bitter is care for companion to him who hath few friends to shield him ... He knows this who is forced to forgo his lord's, his friend's counsels, to lack them for long."

At the bottom of society was the slave, known as the *theow* or bondman, with his hair cut short as a badge of low status. He had no rights of his own and was employed with his wife in his lord's fields in return for food and shelter. He could not leave his master's estate without permission. To do so was to desert and become outcast.

Next up from the slave was the *ceorl* (pronounced "churl") who might have had a small farm close to his lord's farm, where he owed service. He may himself have had a slave and his farm would have been stocked by the lord.

The freeman usually had land of his own which was held for rent and food render – ale, cheese, corn and cattle, which he had to hand over to his lord. He was expected to bear arms for the lord and these were returned to the lord at death. Next to the freeman was the great noble and, above him, his lord, the king.

All were bound to each other. Men owed service and loyalty to their lord and master; he owed them protection, weapons, land and stock. The greater one's lord the greater one's own security. A powerful lord was a blessing in troubled times.

Burial places of the East Angles

Nearly 100 early Anglo-Saxon burial places have been found in East Anglia, mostly by chance during quarrying and building. More are still being discovered. They are extremely important to the archaeologist, revealing vital information about the wealth and social structure of the early settlements.

Cemeteries were very important to the East Angles and they sited them with care. While some cemeteries marked the edge of tribal territories, others may have been near the lord's hall. This could explain why some burial places are close to later villages and churches, as is the case at North Runcton, Swaffham, Hilgay and Caistor St Edmund.

Norfolk's best-known Anglo-Saxon cemetery is at Spong Hill, North Elmham. Abandoned before 600 after a century's use, it contained some 2500 cremation pots and 57 graves. First discovered in 1711, it was completely excavated between 1972-1981.

One of its most elaborate graves may have belonged to a local lord. In it a man was buried with a spear, shield, sword and bucket (possibly a mead bucket, which would have been passed round his feast hall). A burial mound or "barrow" – a clear mark of high status – was raised above the grave. Nearby were the graves of men with spears and shields. They may have been some of his freemen.

Women were buried dressed, wearing brooches and beads, and often with knives and rough pots. One woman of some importance was found with two girdlehangers (large bronze "keys"), amber beads, brooches,

A cremation urn fresh from the ground at Spong Hill; decorated with five stamped designs, this urn is being carefully re-assembled after 1400 years of compaction beneath this Norfolk field. (Michael Dabski, Warsaw University, courtesy of Norfolk Archaeological Unit)

(Left) An unusual, indeed unique, cremation urn lid; the enigmatic and mysterious 'Spong Man'. (Mick Sharp – Norfolk Archaeological Unit)

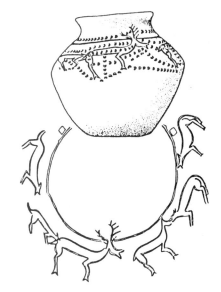

A cremation urn from Spong Hill, with its design extended beneath (above right) and three other animal stamped motifs from the same site (above left).

knives and a bronze bowl. A weaving-batten placed in her grave may indicate that she was in charge of the weaving sheds.

Most Anglo-Saxons at Spong Hill were cremated, their bones placed in special pots with gravegoods and buried singly or in small, possibly family groups. Many of the pots were decorated with lines and stamped impressions. Some are highly distinctive, obviously the work of the same potter or workshop. It is tempting to see magical or religious significance in the designs on some pots. The swastika, a common mark, may have symbolised the god Thor; runes may refer to another, Tiw. One remarkable pot shows a stag and hind cornered by two pairs of hunting dogs.

Burial was probably a public, rather than a private, family affair, with the pagan priest following ancient custom in the ritual.

Two early Saxon posthole buildings being excavated at Spong Hill, North Elmham. (Top: Jean Williamson – Norfolk Archaeological Unit. Bottom: Mick Sharp – Norfolk Archaeological Unit)

(Below) Cruciform gold pendant set with garnets and containing a gold coin of the Byzantine Emperor Heraclius (610-640). From Wilton, near Hockwold.

Animal design from a dress fitting, probably 8th century, from Binham.

(Above left) King David playing a lyre similar to an example excavated from the Bergh Apton cemetery. From a manuscript of the early 8th century.

Gravegoods surely reflected rank and status. A sword was a mark of particularly high status. Freemen were usually buried with spears, shields and knives. Combs and manicure sets of shears, tweezers and razors may also have denoted free people for, as we have seen, the early laws suggest that slaves were identified by short, cropped hair. Tools, oxgoads, spindle-whorls and fragments of bronze bowls may have belonged to craftsmen and tradesmen. All these gravegoods were intended to accompany the dead on their journey after death.

High infant and child mortality is indicated by the cremated remains of numerous children who died as a result of diseases, the rigours of winter or injury. Their bones were often placed in small plain pots, sometimes next to a larger pot containing the remains of an adult.

Considerable variation between cemeteries reflects different local customs and levels of wealth.

At Morningthorpe, where a large cemetery of 400 or more graves has been excavated, almost all burials were unburnt. Like Spong Hill there was wide variation in the quality of gravegoods. Only one grave contained a sword and one other a glass vessel. Many graves had just a knife and buckle and others had no gravegoods at all. The cemetery shows the full range of 6th century East Anglian society, from the nobility to slaves.

One Morningthorpe grave contained the remains of a lyre, a small harp-like musical instrument. Remarkably, another was found in a cemetery a few miles away at Bergh Apton. They almost certainly belonged to scops, who entertained their lords in great halls with songs and poetry.

Kings were normally buried separately, perhaps under barrows in family cemeteries. No royal graves have so far been found in Norfolk. Suffolk was the royal heartland.

Together, the county's cemeteries are showcases of early Anglo-Saxon art. Ornamented objects like brooches and wristclasps bear breathtaking designs of animals and human faces, twisted and folded to fit small panels.

Towards the end of the pagan period in the early 7th century, some of the richest graves show the adoption of a fashion for gold jewellery with glass and garnet inlay. The wealthy were evidently in touch with aristocratic culture in Europe, where the same jewellery was in vogue.

The heathen world

Bede once described a pagan's concept of life as brief, like the flight of a sparrow from the darkness outside through a warm and bright mead hall, full of happy company, and then out into the dark and friendless winter night beyond.

As pagans, the early Anglo-Saxons had no formal theology of an after-life. The dream of the warrior was that his fame would live on after him and be celebrated by future generations. In a similar way, the kings traced their ancestry back to Woden, the war god.

Like the rest of barbarian Europe, the Anglo-Saxons had tribal gods and countless local cults. Kings and lords were themselves cult religious figures. Tribes had many holy places and it was widely believed that individual trees, springs, stones and sacred groves had supernatural powers.

The north Norfolk village of Matlaske, the name of which means moot ash, may have begun as a pagan meeting place. Elmham and

Ashmanhaugh are likely to have been named after sacred trees. Ellough, meaning temple hill, is a reminder of the temples where priests performed pagan rites.

The early Anglo-Saxons were superstitious farmers who offered sacrifices through the seasons to protect their crops, animals and good luck.

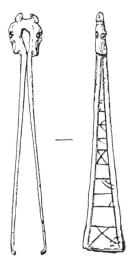

(Left) A pair of bronze tweezers from Heacham. The runic inscription has no meaning.

(Above right) Runes found cut on a sheep ankle-bone in a cremation urn at Caistor St Edmund. The runes are meaningless in the order that they have been cut, but may be rearranged to produce the Anglo-Saxon words 'neah' (near) and 'hwaer' (where). Their true meaning might be lost for ever.

(Left) A stamped design on a Spong Hill cremation urn. The letter 'T' shown in three ways is possibly an evocation of the god Tiw.

In February, known as Solmonth, cakes were offered to the gods. March was the festival of Hretha, a god of fertility, while April was Eostur month, named after the spring goddess Eostre. In September, holy month, sacrifices were made at the end of the harvest (our harvest festival). November, then known as blood-month, saw the slaughter of surplus cattle. Yuletide, the festival to mark the end of the year, included the celebration of Mother's Night – December 25th.

Of all their gods, the Anglo-Saxons held Woden to be the most important; he was the war god, protector of the lord's hall and warriors, and the lord of fire and lightning. Human sacrifices, possibly by hanging, were carried out in his name. Woden's symbols included the wolf, raven, eagle, spear and whetstone. The whetstones found occasionally in burials may have been offerings to Woden.

Another war god, Thor, was the noble and powerful god for all men. Fertility, marriage and children were the realm of Freyr, whose symbols were the horse and the boar. Tiw was a sky god whose name was carved in runes on swords to ensure victory (Anglo-Saxon freemen often made oaths on their weapons).

Some of the symbols associated with the gods are even seen on cemetery pots. They were either intended as magical symbols or to invoke the gods. The swastika, a common symbol, represents Thor. One pot from Spong Hill bears the rune for Tiw impressed by a special stamp. A remarkable pot from Caistor St Edmund shows the Anglo-Saxon legend ship Naglfar, with a crew of giants and the wolf Fenrir. In the legend, the ship is made from the nails of dead men.

Anglo-Saxons believed that the powers of darkness were controlled by invisible elves and demons which caused ills and diseases. Because man's fate was seen as resting in the hands of the gods, they sought to defeat and placate the elves and demons to secure good luck.

Christianity, already adopted by the "civilised" world, brought an entirely different message and cast aside all the old superstitions (though it took over many of the old festivals). Its gospel taught that the sorrows of this life were as nothing to the hopes of eternal life.

The spread of Christianity was resisted by many Anglo-Saxons, who still nursed old Germanic customs. Even when Anglo-Saxon kings and their courts had embraced the new religion, the ways of paganism were not easily abandoned. Conversion to Christ was a slow, fitful process.

Halls, huts and potsherds

Throughout Anglo-Saxon times almost all buildings were of wood. Apart from a few stone churches, which may date from the very end of the period, no Anglo-Saxon buildings survive above ground in Norfolk. Any traces of houses, workshops and agricultural buildings consist of discolourations in the soil. Wood survives only under unusual circumstances, such as waterlogging.

The first Anglo-Saxon building in Norfolk to be excavated, at Postwick in the 1930s, was thought at the time to be pre-Roman Iron Age. Since then, knowledge of Anglo-Saxon buildings has advanced and many settlements have been successfully excavated.

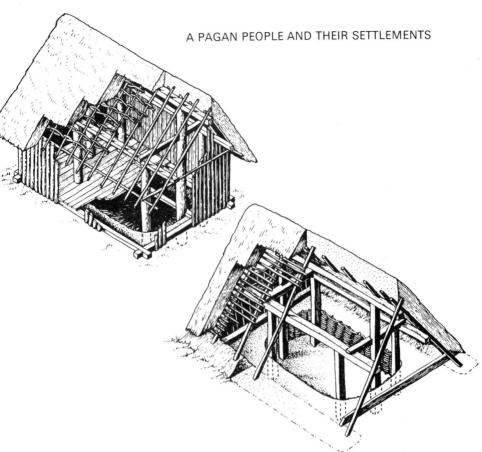

The two interpretations of the Early Saxon 'sunken featured' building: a pit below a tent-like roof (right) or a more roomy structure with under-floor storage facilities (above).

The most common building type in the 5th to 7th centuries was the "sunken-featured building" or Grubenhaus, brought from the continent. Surviving evidence consists of a level-based pit, usually rectangular, with one or more posts at either end (which are evidence of walls and a roof).

Much controversy has centred on whether the floor of the structure was on the pit base or on planks suspended across it. These alternatives make a great deal of difference to any reconstruction of the buildings' original appearance.

At West Stow, where a large part of an early Anglo-Saxon settlement has been excavated, both types have been used in the reconstruction of several buildings.

Most people would describe a structure where the floor is at the base of the pit as a hut or hovel. The more plausible floor-over-pit building would have been both airy and habitable and capable of being used for a variety of functions, including a living house, weaving shed and craft workshop. The "sunken-featured building" leaves obvious traces in the soil and is thus commonly found in small-scale salvage excavations.

By contrast, timber structures with wall-posts set in the ground, either in post-holes, slots or trenches, are far more difficult for the archaeologist to recognise. Yet they are found on all sites excavated with the aid of modern techniques. In general these buildings were larger than the sunken-featured buildings, and although little is known of their purpose a domestic use seems likely. Some may have been the halls referred to in Anglo-Saxon literature.

Fine series of such timber-structured houses have been excavated at Spong Hill (6th century), in North Elmham village (8th-9th century) and at Thetford (10th-11th century). The best preserved structures of all have recently been uncovered on a never-ploughed site at Brandon, just over the border in Suffolk. There, on an island in the river valley, more than 20 buildings of the 8th and 9th centuries have been found with intact floors, usually of trampled earth and with a layer of occupation debris above. Finds from this layer indicate the various activities carried out within the buildings. This settlement, in a remote spot, was probably a monastery.

Archaeologists have little idea of the varying size and status of each settlement because none has been completely excavated. More investigation is needed before it is known whether the sites were individual farms, hamlets, villages or straggling settlements. The problems are compounded by a marked tendency for Anglo-Saxon settlements to move, shrink, coalesce and disaggregate.

In an effort to explain this settlement shift, work has been under way for some years on the Norfolk silt fenland and on parishes such as Hales, Heckingham and Loddon in the east and Barton Bendish in the west. This work consists of plotting fragments of pottery found on the surfaces of ploughed fields. These humble fragments are usually the only surface indication of Anglo-Saxon habitation, and can be dated to establish when each site was founded, how long it was occupied and when it was deserted for a new site elsewhere.

It was not until the later 11th-12th centuries that settlements grew up that have remained on the same sites to become the villages of today. Many of the latter, however, have been on their present sites since only the 11th or 12th centuries.

BIRTH OF A KINGDOM

The royal dynasty of the Wuffingas

Many early Anglo-Saxon kingdoms were unstable, their rule being shared or contested between branches of royal families and their peace shattered by feuds. Struggles within a dynasty could lead to death or exile, even for close relatives. Relations with the dynasties of other kingdoms were sometimes good, sometimes bad. They often led to war but were always intimate. After all, kings needed each other and were always trying to make allies and gain promises of support.

The East Angles were fortunate in having an orderly succession of rulers drawn from the Wuffinga dynasty. Raedwald, the most powerful king of his day, was the dynasty's best-known leader.

The Wuffingas are believed to have been descended from a wave of Scandinavian invaders who settled in the region in about 500. King Wehha was later remembered as "the first to rule over the East Angles in Britain," probably around 550, and his son, Wuffa, gave his name to the royal line. Wuffa's son, Tyttla, succeeded him and on his death in 599 his son, Raedwald, came to the throne.

Raedwald at a Christian court

Before his accession, Raedwald was a guest (perhaps even an exile) in the household of Ethelbert of Kent, the pagan chief king of southern England. Through his marriage to the Christian princess Bertha (a Frank), Ethelbert became sympathetic to Christianity. In 597 Pope Gregory the Great used him to bring Britain back into Christendom by sending a mission, led by Augustine, of 40 monks, a unique event which created special links between England and Rome.

The mission came to Kent, the closest kingdom to the Franks and, thanks to Ethelbert's active support, it succeeded. Some 10,000 people were baptised at Christmas 597. Ethelbert even persuaded Raedwald to adopt Christianity, but his influence was transient. Bede records that on returning to East Anglia to become king, Raedwald was "led astray" by his pagan wife, adding: "He had in the same temple an altar for the holy sacrifice of Christ side-by-side with an altar on which victims were offered to the devil." Perhaps he was not strong enough to offend his wife and nation and risk losing their support by adopting the new faith wholeheartedly.

Raedwald's rise to supremacy

A relapsed Christian, Raedwald increased his power dramatically in 616 following a battle in Northumbria. Ethelfrith, the Northumbrian king, bribed Raedwald to murder Edwin, a fugitive claimant to his throne who was sheltering in East Anglia. Influenced by his pagan wife, who wondered how "so great a king could sell his friend for gold," Raedwald kept his honour by refusing to kill him, and leading his troops north to defeat Ethelfrith and claim his kingdom. Raedwald's son, Ragenhere, was killed in the conflict.

Edwin, owing Raedwald so much, was installed as the client king in Northumbria. The victory ensured Raedwald's supremacy among English kings and established him as Bretwalda, or "chief ruler."

Sutton Hoo: the burial of a king

Little else was known of Raedwald until his probable burial place was discovered at Sutton Hoo, Suffolk, in 1939. A huge barrow containing the remains of a great ship, nearly 90 feet long, was excavated on a bluff overlooking the river Deben. It had been dragged up a hill from the river below and its cargo of kingly treasures was still intact.

With its rich gravegoods and weapons, the burial was a powerful symbol of the aristocratic elite and a reminder that the East Angles had origins in Scandinavia, where numerous ship burials have been found.

Excavators discovered no trace of a human burial. The body was either destroyed by the acidity of the soil or buried elsewhere, with the ship representing a cenotaph. Archaeologists now believe that traces of a body would almost certainly have been discovered if modern excavation techniques had been used.

The unsurpassed craftsmanship of many of the gravegoods indicates they were made by a workshop attached to Raedwald's court. An elaborately-carved whetstone, a possible symbol of Thor, is thought to be a "sceptre." Raedwald's life in his feast hall is reflected in the silver-mounted drinking horns, wooden bottles, a great cauldron, minstrel's maplewood lyre and mead-bucket.

Raedwald was a warrior, and his weapons were carried to the ship and laid by his side. They included a sword with exquisite gold and garnet belt fittings, a mail coat, a Scandinavian helmet, an axe, spears and a lavish shield, decorated with barbarian designs of eagles, boars, horses and entwined animals.

The excavated material shows how barbarian kings in the west had adopted many of the fashions of the rest of the known world. An Egyptian bowl and a large silver dish from Byzantium, already 200 years old when buried, were among the gravegoods. The small stag and mounts on the sceptre may even come from the nomadic people of central Asia.

Objects of startling Christian significance were laid among the pagan gravegoods – 10 silver bowls, chased with delicate crosses, and two silver spoons, perhaps Raedwald's christening gifts from Ethelbert.

Through his friends in Kent Raedwald had links with the Franks in Gaul. A magnificent purse unearthed at Sutton Hoo contained 40 gold coins, each from a different Frankish mint. These may have been for the 40 rowers of that great ship. The coins were minted sometime between 621 and 629 – a strong indication that the ship burial was indeed the cenotaph or final resting place of Raedwald, who died in 624.

Enamelled decorative mount from a seventh-century Hanging-Bowl found at Hindringham. The mount is bronze, the enamel (stippled) is red. The design is similar to those on Irish metalwork. The two pierced holes show that it was re-used as a pendant.

A hanging-bowl (based on an example from the Sutton Hoo ship-burial). Hanging-Bowls are sometimes found in high-class Anglo-Saxon graves, But seem to be of Celtic design and manufacture.

THE TRIUMPH OF CHRISTIANITY

The royal church

After Raedwald's death the power of East Anglia waned. His protege, King Edwin of Northumbria, took over as Bretwalda (England's most powerful king) and another of Raedwald's sons, Eorpwald, became king of East Anglia.

Initially a pagan, Edwin accepted Christianity in 627 and immediately set about converting Eorpwald. Bede comments that Eorpwald was persuaded to "abandon his superstitious idolatry and accept the faith and sacraments of Christ with his whole province." Eorpwald became Edwin's "godson" and links between the two kingdoms were strengthened, with East Anglia now the "client" kingdom.

Later in the same year, however, Eorpwald was killed by Ricbert, a pagan. Sigbert, probably a stepson of Raedwald whom Bede describes as "a good and religious man," then claimed the throne and brought the East Angles permanently to Christianity. Sigbert had little help from the Roman mission but used monks from Ireland and Gaul.

The first bishop

Sigbert welcomed to his kingdom a Burgundian missionary, Felix, who became the first bishop of the East Angles. Felix was established at Dunwich, a coastal settlement now mostly washed away by the sea, and he remained bishop from 630 until his death in 647.

Sigbert and his bishop Felix set up a school "for the education of boys in the study of letters" and appointed the Irish monk Fursa to a monastery at Cnobheresburh, either Burgh Castle, the old Roman shore fort, or possibly Caister-on-Sea.

Sigbert then retired to a monastery to devote himself, in the words of Bede, "to winning an everlasting kingdom."

The Mercian threat

Bede preferred strong kings to pious ones, believing that their strength guaranteed the safety of the church. When in 636, following the death of

Edwin, the pagan prince Penda, a belligerent Mercian, viciously attacked East Anglia, he faced Sigbert, by then a monk. The once-noble warrior was dragged from his cell to lead an army but refused to carry any weapon except his staff. Not surprisingly he was slain.

Strangely, Penda did not conquer East Anglia and the kingdom passed in turn to Raedwald's three nephews, who all had to withstand the pagan threat of Mercia. Cnobheresburh, probably Burgh Castle or Caister on Sea, for example, was attacked and abandoned.

King Anna, described by Bede as a saintly man, succeeded to the East Anglian throne in 636 and was killed 18 years later opposing Penda. His hapless brother Ethelhere had even less luck. He met his end fighting *for* Penda. A sub-king and unwilling ally, he and Penda died in a great battle against Oswiu of Northumbria in 655.

Although Penda was pagan his quarrels and campaigns were not about religion and many of his allies were Christian. His prime motivation was to carve out a territory for himself.

Anna's other brother, Ethelwald, ruled East Anglia until 662 and was followed by the long reigns of two quite obscure kings, Aldwulf (circa 663-713) and Alfwald (circa 713-749).

King Anna and his daughters

As well as securing everlasting fame by dying at the hands of the pagan Penda, Anna is well known for his four saintly daughters, whose lives epitomised the aristocratic ideal.

The eldest, Sexburga, married a Kentish king and founded a nunnery at Sheppey in Kent. Etheldreda, the best known, married Tondbert, a prince of a Fenland tribe who appears to have died shortly after the wedding.

Against her will Etheldreda was remarried, to King Egfrith of Northumbria, but she refused to consummate the union. With the encouragement of Bishop Wilfred she held on to her virginity for 12 years, resisting all her husband's advances in the hope of becoming a nun.

Perhaps in desperation, Egfrith finally allowed her to become a nun and she returned to East Anglia in 673 to found a monastery at Ely (the first nunnery in eastern England). When she died in 679 her sister Sexburga, by then a widow, succeeded her as abbess of the monastery.

At Deorham, probably West Dereham and not East Dereham, as is usually assumed, another of Anna's daughters, Withburga, established a small monastery on the Fen edge.

Anna's was a remarkably pious family. When he was killed in 654 his body was taken to his own monastery at Blythburgh to rest in the care of the monks. Both Anna's widow and his other daughter Ethelburga became abbesses at a French nunnery. It is possible that the remote monastery at Iken, Suffolk, built in the same year on an island in the marshes of the river Alde, was established to commemorate Anna. His brothers, Ethelhere and Ethelwald, were patrons of this isolated but important religious community.

Private monasteries

By the end of the 7th century the founding of "private" monasteries was an expression of aristocratic piety. Having adopted Christianity, the nobility built its own churches and sent its offspring to Gaul to be educated. The sons and especially the daughters of the nobility formed a closely-knit group with contacts across kingdom boundaries. Towards the ends of their lives kings (such as Sigbert) and queens often retreated to their monasteries, like Iken and Brandon.

As the monasteries proliferated Bede complained bitterly that many were false, loose-living establishments, "useful neither to God nor man." Even after the English church was reorganised and regularised in the 660s, private monasteries continued, free of bishops' control and often little more than high-class households.

There is a remarkable lack of known early monasteries (both private and "regular") in Norfolk. Doubtless they existed, but the Danish invasions of the 9th century and later destroyed both the monasteries and their records. Monasteries were sometimes set up in remote spots, often in river valleys on virtual "islands," thought to symbolise their separation from the everyday world. It is possible that early foundations existed at Hickling, St Benet's and at Wormegay, in addition to West Dereham and Brandon.

The great dykes

An impressive sight for travellers to East Anglia is the series of five dry dykes running from the Fen edge to the borders of the kingdom of Essex, each consisting of banks on one side, the north east, and ditches on the other, the south west. They are certainly post-Roman and appear to be Saxon in date. They surely mark the boundary of the Anglo-Saxon East Anglian kingdom.

The largest, Devil's Dyke, is some 12 miles long and resembles a railway embankment in parts. Fine stretches can be seen at Reach and near

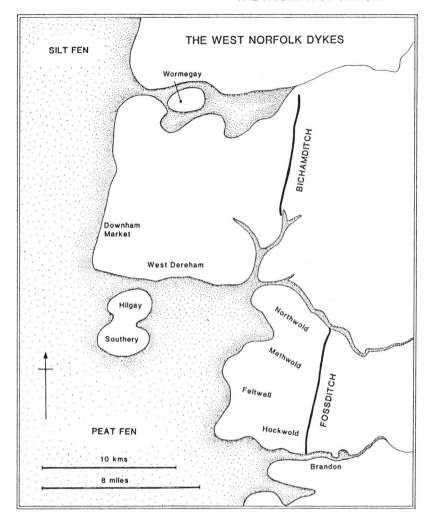

THE WEST NORFOLK DYKES

SILT FEN

Wormegay

BICHAMDITCH

Downham Market

West Dereham

Hilgay

Southery

Northwold

Methwold

Feltwell

FOSSDITCH

PEAT FEN

Hockwold

Brandon

10 kms

8 miles

The West Norfolk dykes cutting off two 'peninsulas' which jut out into the Fenland between the mouths of the Rivers Nar, Wissey and Little Ouse.

Newmarket. Why these massive earthworks were constructed is something of a mystery.

A great king with huge resources, possibly Raedwald, could have built them to mark the frontiers of his territory and to control the movement of cattle and armies.

In Norfolk other dykes, now much reduced in size but still impressive, are thought to mark the boundaries of minor territories or "estates."

Bicham Ditch, running north-south from Narborough to Beechamwell, forms the east boundary of a large area, with the Fens as the west boundary and the rivers Nar and Wissey to north and south. The area includes Downham Market, Fincham and many other, minor places.

The Foss Ditch is similar, enclosing a large area also bounded by fen and rivers (the Wissey and Little Ouse). This area seems to have been nearly all ancient woods (wolds) – Hockwold, Methwold and Northwold – besides Feltwell and Wilton. This tract of woodland may have been set aside by a powerful king, possibly for hunting.

Of the other dykes in the county, the Launditch in central Norfolk probably dates to the pre-Roman Iron Age, while Panworth Ditch at Ashill, Devil's Dyke at Garboldisham and Bunns Bank south of Attleborough remain of uncertain age.

Devil's Dyke. Swaffham-Downham Market Road, looking north April 1990 (Copyright Poppyland Photos)

TWO QUIET CENTURIES

Gipeswic and Northwic

No towns existed in 6th century England, the remnants of late Roman urban life having disappeared by 500. The return of trade to northern Europe was marked by the establishment of many coastal and riverside trading places called wics.

At some time around 600 a trading settlement was founded at Ipswich, then known as Gipeswic, under the probable control of the Wuffinga dynasty.

Gipeswic became East Anglia's Anglo-Saxon boom town. At first quite small in extent – about 25 acres – it had grown to some 125 acres by the 8th century, spreading south across the river into what is now the suburb of Stoke. In the early centuries the town was open, with no defences.

Trade and manufacturing industry were behind the rise of Gipeswic. Its trading links were almost exclusively with the Rhineland, from where pottery, wine, glass and querns for grinding corn were imported. At Ipswich, archaeological evidence has been found for the manufacture of leather goods, bone implements, bronze objects and pottery.

Ipswich-ware pots were the first to be produced industrially in England since the end of the Roman period. They were so superior to the hand and home-made pots from the rest of East Anglia that they found their way to all parts of the kingdom, and even to Kent and County Durham.

By the late 9th century Ipswich had become a town of regional pre-eminence. Its relative importance subsequently declined and its settled area did not expand significantly until Victorian times.

Ipswich may have been East Anglia's major town before the coming of the Danes at the end of the 9th century. Yet it is not mentioned in documents until the 10th century, after its heyday, and all that is known about its origins and growth has been gleaned from archaeological research.

Norwich (Northwic), first mentioned on a coin of Athelstan in the 930s, has until recently yielded little evidence of pre-Danish occupation. But in 1985 a tiny excavation in Fishergate, north of the river Wensum and east of Magdalen Street, produced more pottery and other finds of the 8th and 9th centuries than all previous digs in the city put together.

Although further excavations will be needed to prove the idea, it is likely that the origins of Norwich as a town lie north of the river, away from the centre of the late Saxon and medieval town.

It is perhaps not too fanciful to see in the name Northwic a trading centre which was named not because it was north of the Wensum but because it lay north of its larger and earlier-founded "mother" settlement, Ipswich.

Besides Ipswich and possibly Norwich, Dunwich in Suffolk – now largely removed by the sea – may have been another East Anglian trading port. It is also conceivable that north-west Norfolk, a heavily-settled area where a wealth of 8th and 9th century material has been found on many rural sites, may have been served by its own port.

Royal control of trade, which had led to the birth of Ipswich, continued after East Anglia fell under Mercian rule in the mid-8th century. If Norwich was emerging during this period it, too, would have been guided by the authority of a Mercian king.

Each *wic* was under the control of a royal reeve, and in return for his special protection the king exacted tolls, rents and fines. Sometimes the king gave away some of his rights and jurisdiction to a church in return for its supervision of quays and markets.

St Martin (at Palace) in Norwich may have been one such church, dominating a quayside market place. St Michael in Tombland would almost certainly have been another. That these two churches existed before late Saxon times we have, of course, no evidence at present. The churches at Norwich's town gates (such as All Saints in Magdalen Street) may have origins as gatekeepers, placed to control entry into the town and to impose tolls on carts coming to market. Two Thetford churches, St Andrew and St Cuthbert, may be other examples, built next to town gates.

The merchants who came to Norwich and Ipswich were under the special protection of the king and had to obey his reeve. On their travels merchants had the king as their "lord" and were responsible to him. Merchants from abroad were expected to change their money into English coinage at the port.

The return of coins

Small silver pieces called sceattas were the earliest distinctively East Anglian coins. A general class of coin without royal names, they circulated throughout southern and eastern England as well as across the North Sea.

East Anglian sceattas were probably minted during the reign of King Aldwulf (circa 663-713). His successor, Alfwald (circa 713-749), seems to have exerted stricter monetary control over his kingdom because the distribution of sceattas mirrored quite closely the extent of his territory.

In the late 750s a shadowy figure called Beonna, who succeeded Alfwald, became the first East Anglian king to issue coins bearing his own name. A hoard of 51 Beonna coins was found recently at Middle Harling near Thetford. Less than 30 have been found elsewhere.

From the time of Beonna in about 760 until the death of the Mercian king Offa in 796, East Anglia was a virtual dependency of Mercia.

The next East Anglian monarch, Ethelred, did not mint coins and his successor, Ethelbert, who was executed by Offa of Mercia in 794, left us only three coins, one of which was found in Rome.

Offa, who introduced the penny, a standard weight coin usually bearing the royal name, did not look kindly on monetary independence on the part of his sub-kings. Throughout the 9th century until the Danish invasion of 869 and the death of King Edmund in 870, coins were struck by East Anglian kings at an unknown mint or mints, first under the dominance of Mercia and later under that of Wessex.

Coins were less widely circulated in Anglo-Saxon England than in Roman Britain. The vast majority of Anglo-Saxons relied on barter and exchange in their daily lives. Royal control of coinage was absolute and was exercised through moneyers, men licensed by royal authority to produce coins. Their names usually appeared on the reverses of the coins.

Anglo-Saxon coins had a good silver content. There were no base metal coins in circulation in southern England. In an age when the bullion value of silver was paramount, coinage was used in the taxation system and for international trade rather than for day-to-day transactions.

New estates for old

Even in the early Anglo-Saxon centuries Norfolk was well populated, extensively cultivated and divided into great estates. As time went by and the population of the region grew the estates began to break up into smaller and still smaller communities. It was a process which gave birth to the medieval parishes we know today.

In the absence of early documents the shape and character of the old great estates can be discerned from the pattern of place names. For example, a cluster of parishes with names ending in -ton – Yelverton, Thurton, Hellington, Claxton and Apton – could hark back to an earlier, mother estate, perhaps Framingham, which may in turn indicate an early tribal group, the Framingas.

The boundaries of the ancient estates were long, often rivers, ridges, Roman roads, heaths and woodlands. Some estates were the territories of obscure tribal groups whilst others were probably controlled by royal families or were in the hands of monasteries.

The central settlements of the old estates were obviously old themselves and usually occurred on the best and most fertile land. Their names were sometimes topographical, referring in the case of Smallburgh to the river Smale (now the Ant). Others had names ending in -ham – Wymondham, Swaffham, Downham, Walsham, Sheringham, Reepham, Stalham, Aylsham, and so on. They often continued as market centres for centuries even as new settlements became established near them.

Wymondham is a particularly good example of how, over several centuries, a big estate was eventually whittled down to nothing more than a large parish. Wymondham now covers more than 10,000 acres, making it one of Norfolk's largest parishes. But even this represents only a small fraction of its former size.

The boundaries of Wymondham's newer, neighbouring estates – places like Wicklewood, Wreningham and Wramplingham – drew ever closer, eating into the fields and woodlands of the old estate.

The increasing importance of boundaries gave rise to the annual Rogationtide procession, when villagers walked round with their priest to beat the bounds of the estate and offer prayers. Apart from its spiritual role, the Rogation procession served the important practical purpose of making villagers familiar with the boundaries of their community.

As we have seen, later settlements frequently had names ending in -ton,

Wymondham: a possible early 'estate' showing its appearance by Late Saxon times, the once dependent settlements now separate vills with their own churches, leaving a still large central 'estate' (now the parish of Wymondham) with its church.

examples including Tacolneston, Buxton, Thurlton, Houghton and Cawston. The character of particular farms is recorded in the names of Barton (meaning barley-ton) Roydon (rye hill) and Wheatacre. Settlements near meadows (then known as *edisc* or *laes*) are Brockdish (meaning brook meadow), Edgefield (edisc field), Lynford (flax ford), Strawless and Beccles.

Much of the countryside developed as a result of the gradual colonisation of the poorer soils and woods of the great estates. The -steads (Tunstead, Worstead, Horstead and Irstead) may be the subsidiary farms established in woods and waste areas.

The summer huts and sheds of woodland grazing grounds also grew into permanent communities. The name of Scole is derived from the old Norse word *skali*, meaning huts. Old wood pastures are signalled by Holt, Gaywood, Woodton, Wootton, Ryston, Mousehold (mouse-holt) Heath and Northwold, Methwold and Hockwold (wold meaning wood).

Clearings (leys) in the woods, where herdsmen lived in huts, are remembered in Foxley, Gateley (goat-ley), Langley (long-ley) and Hardley (herd-ley). New land taken in from waste (brecks and rodes) became Breckles and Carlton Rode. The dairy farms (wicks and stokes) became Hardwick (herd-wick) and Stoke Holy Cross.

By late Saxon times many of the new estates had become independent entities with their own halls, demesne and churches, which often still owed allegiance to the mother church at the heart of the old estate (such as Wymondham Abbey). The new estates were the holdings of freemen and their tenants. Peasants were often allowed to settle outlying woodland areas, paying rent to the lord in return.

In time, some of the new estates were sub-divided. This happened in the cases of East, West and South Raynham, Great and Little Dunham and North and South Creake, to name a few.

Estate life

Anglo-Saxon society was held together by subtle social relationships. The king expected loyalty from his noblemen, lavish hospitality when he visited their halls and a ready supply of armed men to fight his battles. In return, he defended his people.

Like the king, the lord was expected to protect those who lived on his estate. In return for housing, land and stock his tenants and peasants repaired his hall, ploughed and harvested his fields and maintained his estate. Lord, tenant and peasant were also bound together by ancient customs, the great festivals and the routine of the agricultural calendar. A lord and his household would live off the food render from his tenants and peasants and an early law shows that royal estates owed the king honey, loaves, ale, cows, sheep, hens, cheese, butter, fish, eels and even fodder for his horses.

Spring was the time for ploughing, digging ditches and sowing barley, beans and flax. In summer the peasant was expected to set and lay hedges, make hurdles and repair enclosures around common meadows. At harvest the peasants gathered in the barley, oats, wheat and rye, consuming much food and drink as they did so. After the harvest came threshing, thatching and further ploughing and sowing wheat.

Towards the end of the year barns and stalls were prepared for herds of cattle and pigs, which were driven in from the woods for the winter. Some were killed for the winter sacrifice while others were salted down for the long winter ahead.

By preference, the Anglo-Saxons cultivated light soils but they were also pastoral farmers who needed woods for grazing. Much woodland, then mostly of oak and lime, had grown back since Roman times, and the animals were driven to the pastures from homefarms along woodways, or droveroads.

So important was woodland that Saxon kings took steps to protect it and punish those who, by stealth, burned down trees for clearance. For example, a harsh fine of 60 shillings was imposed for "cutting down a tree which could shelter 30 swine." By custom, peasants were only allowed to take wood that could be reached "by hook or by crook." Villages sometimes shared woodland grazing; other areas were set aside as royal hunting grounds.

In the depths of the woods, far from human habitation, the swineherd might come face to face with wild boar, bears, wolves and other wild animals. Beavers and small deer were common and many a peasant-pot must have been graced by venison, taken illicitly by the herdsmen.

Around the huts of the homestead children, cats, dogs, chickens and geese ran free. Older children watched over grazing pigs in distant wood pastures.

Sheep, then the most numerous animals, were run on fen and open heath. They were kept mainly for their wool rather than their meat. Cattle were also kept, grazing in meadows and woodland. They were valuable beasts and, as easy measures of wealth, were the targets of raids and rustlers.

In the fields, oxen were used to draw ploughs. Teams of them were jointly owned by freemen or owned and let out by the lord. The horse, regarded as a noble animal, was reserved for riding. Only in late Saxon times did it become available to those outside the nobility. The lord's hall and household was the heart of the estate. To his barns came the food-rents and renders. Attached to the hall were the craftsmen –

carpenters, blacksmiths, millwrights, shoemakers – working under a reeve, who also supervised buying and selling.

This exchange of goods led to the development of markets, which often took place in churchyards on Sundays when people were gathered together. The first churches were invariably built near the hall. In some places, landowners, perhaps in rivalry, built their own churches in order to be deemed "thegn-worthy," providing two or more churches in a single village or yard. Examples include Barton Bendish, Great Melton, South Walsham and Reepham, where three churches stood in the same churchyard in the Middle Ages.

All roads usually led to the lord's hall at the centre of the estate. The hall also served as a court where justice was dispensed under the eye of the priest.

Before the growth of towns in the later 9th century the production of bronze, bone and wooden objects, as well as of pottery and textiles, was carried out in rural settlements. Early and middle Saxon villages and hamlets were at least partly self-sufficient, with many products made "in-house." Archaeological evidence for these activities is frequently recovered from countryside excavations.

With the foundation of towns much of this industry became urban-based, although blacksmiths still found work in most rural settlements. The pottery industry, which flourished in Norwich and Thetford, has left us the most durable and obvious evidence of Anglo-Saxon industry. Towards the end of the Saxon period there was a return of pottery production to the countryside. Kiln sites have been found at a number of places, including Great Bircham, Langhale, Fransham and, most notably, Grimston.

Another rural industry to have left traces of its existence is iron ore extraction, which was at its most intense on the Cromer Ridge around Sheringham and Weybourne. There, the landscape is pockmarked with mining pits and littered with slag, the residue of the smelting process.

The largest man-made features in Norfolk which pre-date the modern period are the Broads, which were dug to provide peat for domestic and industrial heating. It is certain that the bulk of this peat digging took place in medieval times, but there is a strong possibility that work was well under way by the end of the Saxon period.

The Fens

The desolate wilderness of the Norfolk Fenland was almost devoid of human occupation in early Saxon times. The area was divided into the "black" or peat fen to the south and the silt fen or Marshland to the north, around the edge of the Wash.

In the Roman period much of the western part of the silt fen was settled by communities of farmers and salt producers, but in the 5th century inundations by the sea buried the Roman landscape under a layer of silt. The peat fen was inhabited in Saxon times, although evidence of the early Saxon origins of Hilgay and Southery, each on an island within the Fens, has recently come to light.

A massive archaeological field survey of Marshland in the mid-1980s by Bob Silvester located only one site of early Saxon date. A meagre collection of pottery fragments was found at Tilney St Lawrence on top of an abandoned silted canal built in the Roman period.

Sometime in the 8th century settlement took place on a large scale. A series of middle Saxon communities was founded on low banks of silt, or "roddens," which marked the meanderings of long-extinct watercourses in an arc stretching from Walsoken in the south-west up through Walpole and Terrington, and then down to Tilney.

Evidence suggests that the positioning of these sites was planned, for they occur at regular intervals across the fen. Although they are at present known from surface scatters only (no excavation having taken place), it is certain that the settlements represented a huge colonisation over a relatively short period.

Ground conditions were too wet for extensive arable farming so stock rearing, using the rich grasses that abound on newly-desalinated land, must have been the mainstay of the economy. One notable characteristic of the sites was the density of animal bone scatters, indicating that meat exports to the Norfolk and Suffolk uplands were the source of the Marshlanders' wealth.

One of the sites, at Hay Green, Terrington St Clement, was truly huge, spreading along a system of roddens for about a mile. This site and the others were unusually prolific in mostly Ipswich-ware pottery.

Though impossible to prove, it is likely that the arc of settlements, with its regular spacing, its preoccupation with meat production and its plentiful supply of Ipswich pottery, may have grown up under the control of some powerful authority, probably royal.

Some of the middle Saxon settlements had died out by the end of the 9th century, while others had shrunk and others had moved. A great disruption had occurred, and it is tempting to link it with Viking raids.

Many of the late Saxon settlements lie underneath the modern villages and it was probably in the 10th and 11th centuries that the Sea Bank, mistakenly dubbed Roman in the 17th century, was constructed by villagers to protect their homes and lands from the sea.

At the time of the Norman Conquest Marshland was unremarkable in the size of its population and wealth but by the 13th century it was again a rich and densely-settled region.

(Above) An animal in a twist, showing the Anglo-Saxons' love of intertwining beasts. A gilt silver mount from a woman's grave at Morningthorpe.

(Right) A silver dress fastener of the 9th century. The animal motif is picked out on a background of niello (black silver oxide).

Obscure kings

From circa 750 to 825, East Anglia was under the heel of the powerful kingdom of Mercia, whose rulers tolerated no opposition and fiercely suppressed revolts in subject kingdoms.

Throughout the 8th and most of the 9th centuries, events in East Anglia are almost lost to us and the names of kings are known mainly from coins. As little more than client rulers, they owed Mercia tribute and obedience and could not even grant land to the church without permission.

An example of Mercian ruthlessness came in 794, when King Offa summarily beheaded Ethelbert of East Anglia on some small pretext, perhaps for daring to mint coins in his own name. Offa stamped out any challenge to his rule. His successors, though powerful, were unable to hold down growing rebellion.

Mercian domination was ended in 825 by Athelstan I of East Anglia with West Saxon support. He rebelled against King Beornwulf, killing him and making the East Angles free people again. Thereafter, East Anglia appears to have been allied to Wessex.

IMPACT OF THE DANES: EAST ANGLIA INTO ENGLAND

Early Raids

Amidst the rivalry of East Anglia and Mercia a new threat to peace had arisen in western Europe. Viking long boats had started to raid the coasts of mainland Europe and Britain.

The Scandinavian Vikings, mostly Danes, had for long been traders. Now their sails heralded fearsome attacks on undefended settlements. Great kings were forced to defend their coasts and towns. Mercian kings repaired the Roman walls of Cambridge and may even have built the first earth defences at Norwich to protect the trading town.

The first Viking raids, around the year 800, were against unprotected and isolated targets, especially wealthy monasteries. Monks, so often the victims, recorded the attacks. One wrote: ...the ravages of heathen men miserably destroyed God's church on Lindisfarne.''

The raids died away as the Vikings turned their attention to France, but a new generation saw them return in strength from 835. Each summer brought Viking fleets to English coasts and rivers. From 851 the Vikings remained over winter in camps.

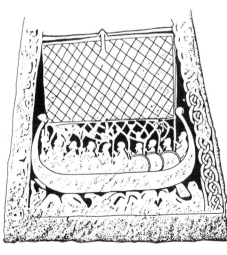

A picture stone from Denmark vividly portrays the maritime might of the Viking invaders.

King Edmund, saint and martyr

King after king gave way to the Vikings, either submitting to their demands or being driven out or killed. Even the mighty Mercians bought peace. As they took over successive kingdoms the Vikings often installed puppet kings. Some were drawn from the families of the kings they had usurped.

When first attacked by the Vikings in 865 the East Anglian King Edmund (855-869) paid tribute and gave supplies to be rid of an army which was probably led by Ubba and Ivar the Boneless, the sons of Ragnar Lothbrok.

Then, in 869, according to the Chronicle, the "raiding army rode across Mercia into East Anglia and took up winter quarters at Thetford. And that winter (in November) King Edmund fought against them, and the Danes had the victory, and killed the king and conquered all the land."

According to other, later sources, the Vikings built a camp at Thetford; Edmund bravely resisted them but was captured and put to death after refusing to share his kingdom and pay tribute. A Christian, he could not yield to a pagan power. His ritual execution – his head was cut off and thrown into a wood at Bradfield, near Bury St Edmunds – secured him swift fame; he became Edmund, saint and martyr.

Edmund's death brought the line of East Anglia's native kings to a sad and violent end. There followed 50 years of Viking control, exercised by kings of whom little is known. It is thought that Viking peasants and warriors settled in East Anglia and made it in many ways a Danish province.

However, those who settled were soon converted to Christianity and within 20 years were issuing pennies in the name of Saint Edmund, whom they had murdered.

A 'Saint Edmund Memorial' coin. These silver pennies, struck to commemorate the martyrdom of the last East Anglian King, were produced, possibly at Thetford, in the late 9th and early 10th centuries.

The Kilverstone stirrup; inlaid with a bronze scroll, this was probably made in Eastern England to a Viking form.

47

Anglo-Saxon Thetford

Thetford was possibly as big or bigger than either Norwich or Ipswich in the late 9th century. Although nearly land-locked, it had connections with the sea and grew in size and importance from 869, becoming a busy port and market town.

Excavation has shed light on the life of the town, which was established on both sides of the river Ouse around an important crossing place on the ancient Icknield Way. Each part of the town was enclosed by earth banks and ditches.

Goods were brought to Thetford along Fenland rivers from such places as St Neots and Stamford. Fishing boats, too, came up river with sea and freshwater fish. Thetford's bustling riverside must have echoed to merchants' and fishermen's voices and the sounds of shipwrights at work.

Thetford in Late Saxon times showing the known layout with possible defences, known roads, and churches.

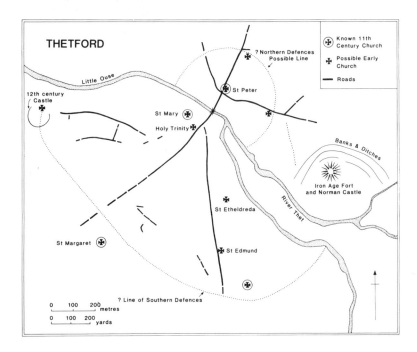

Thetford: an aerial photograph taken in 1956 before massive expansion changed the town. The old London road runs right through the town (bottom left to top right) across the bridge over the Little Ouse which winds through the town. The Iron Age fort enclosing the later Norman castle-mound is bottom right. Red Castle (12th century) is extreme left, hidden in the trees. (Crown Copyright/RAF)

Archaeologists have found parts of folding balances (weighing devices used by merchants and traders). Gravelled roads have been uncovered beside wooden houses, built within fenced plots.

Thetford's Anglo-Saxon inhabitants lived mostly out of doors away from the smoke of the house, only coming in on cold and wet days. All the evidence suggests that Thetford was a dirty, smelly and noisy place, full of industry and animals.

A vast pottery industry grew up in the early 10th century, specialising in high-class wheel-made pottery known to archaeologists as Thetford-ware. Potters' yards and kilns have been found. In one area some kilns were grouped together, possibly representing a single "factory" or production unit. Nearby was space for fuel, piles of clay and a huge water pot sunk into the ground.

Potters would have had to bring their wood and clay from some distance, probably in an oxen-drawn cart. No houses were found near the kilns. The potters must therefore have lived away from their workplace. The smoke and dirt from the kilns would have been considerable; kilns were bad neighbours and tended to be on the edges of towns. Pollution was a problem even then.

Thetford had other industries besides pottery. Textile manufacture, spinning and weaving are suggested by finds of pinbeaters, spindlewhorls, needles, pins, linen smoothers and woolcombs. One very long structure uncovered by excavators may have been a tentering frame for stretching cloth.

Large numbers of sheep, kept on the heaths near Thetford, supplied raw material to the textile trade. Linen was made from locally-grown flax, possibly cultivated at Lynford, the name of which, as we have seen, means flaxford.

Bone was used in many crafts. Bone spoons have been found, as have bone flutes and even bone skates, which were tied to the feet by leather thongs for winter use on the ice of the river and ponds.

Other finds have included numerous crucibles, used in bronze and silver working, a mould for making bronze brooches (which hints at the presence of metal working) and iron tools, including chisels and punches.

The Vikings were fond of skating, and many bone skates, fashioned from animal bones, have been found on Viking sites, notably at Thetford.

A selection of industrially produced Thetford ware pots; jars for cooking, pitchers, storage jars, bowls, lamps, and dishes, all were produced in hard grey earthenware at Thetford and Norwich, and a number of smaller centres, from the late 9th to the end of the 11th century.

Evidence has also been found for leather working. Thetford's economy was supported by a plethora of interdependent tradesmen and craftsmen. Carpenters built the town's houses, mills and even its many churches. They also made the carts needed to bring goods to market. Examples of their workmanship rarely survive, but some of their tools, adzes, saws and metal bits, remain. Iron ore was smelted in several parts of the town. The blacksmith was another crucially important craftsmen, making tools, shoeing horses and finishing wheels. Iron smelting and smithing is evidenced by finds of iron slag, an indestructible by-product that the inhabitants sometimes put to good use as road metalling.

Danish influence in East Anglia

Great social changes took place in the half century of Danish rule and settlement from 870 to 917. The sudden coming of Danish rule prompted a breakdown in the structure of society, disjointing traditional patterns of hierarchy.

Old allegiances to king, bishop and lord were replaced by notions of personal freedom as more and more people gradually became "freemen" with their own small estates. Many English lords were dispossessed or reduced in power, but how many is uncertain.

Before 870, land could only be transferred with the king's charter. Under Danish influence it could be bought and sold in front of witnesses in the chief towns of East Anglia – Cambridge, Thetford, Norwich and Ipswich. Once acquired it could more easily be divided between heirs.

It is not known how many Danish settlers came to East Anglia. Many of the hallmarks of Danish rule appear to date from the reign of Cnut a century later. But while few major place names are Danish, countless minor names – of woods, fields and streams – suggest a strong influence.

The names of two Danish people, Topi and Orm, appear in Topcroft (Topi's croft) and Ormesby (Orm's settlement). The streets of Norwich are "gates," derived from the Danish word *gata*, meaning street. Examples include Colegate, Fishergate, Pottergate and Mountergate.

Danish influence is also seen in place names containing -thorpe (Gunthorpe, Felthorpe), -toft (Toftrees, Toftwood) and -by (Rollesby, Billockby), and also in Thwaite (meaning clearing).

The Danish words for wood, *sco* and *lund*, occur in Sco Ruston and Poringland. Colkirk and Howe are derived from the words for church, *kirk*, and hill *how*. *Beck*, Danish for stream, and *sty*, meaning path, are commonly used.

For all their influence the settlers swiftly adopted the language and religion of the English and abandoned pagan customs.

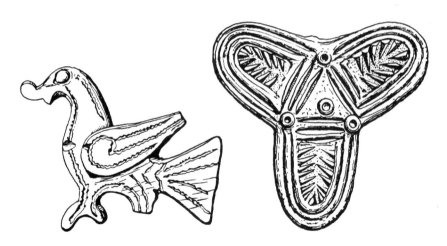

(Above left) A late Viking bird-shaped bronze brooch from Stoke Holy Cross.

(Above right) A typically Viking bronze 'trefoil' brooch from Middle Harling.

The West Saxon conquest of East Anglia

Danish control of East Anglia, which stretched as far west as Northampton, was ended by the vigorous campaigning of Edward the Elder of Wessex, the West Saxon king and son of Alfred the Great.

In 917, according to the Chronicle (the West Saxon record of events), "King Edward went with the army of the West Saxons to Colchester, and repaired and restored the borough where it had been broken. And many people who had been under the rule of the Danes both in East Anglia and in Essex submitted to him; and all the army in East Anglia swore agreement with him ... that they would keep peace with all with whom the king wished to keep peace, both at sea and on land."

East Anglians may have resisted Edward the Elder, not wishing to be absorbed into the great West Saxon empire. After 917 there certainly seems to have been a reluctance on the part of Edward to allow East Anglia any independence.

For example, the region became part of the diocese of London, was ruled by an ealdorman from Wessex and was not given its own bishop for many years. Wessex appears to have suppressed any East Anglian aspirations for self identity and independence.

To hold down and protect his new conquests, Edward improved his defences and built new forts, called burhs, at strategic places to control important river crossings. A burh was built at Bedericsworth (Bury St Edmunds) and the relics of Edmund were moved there to a temporary wooden church as the focus of the new fort on the river Lark.

The conquering West Saxons probably built the first defences at Bungay on a steep spur dominating the river Waveney. The defences controlled the river crossing of the Roman road, which was diverted through the burh and then over the river on a defensive causeway, Ditchingham Dam, which blocked the river to boats.

The defences at Sudbury may also have been the work of Edward. It is possible that at Norwich and Thetford, where there may have been double defensive enclosures on either side of rivers, Edward created new "English" burhs (as he did at Cambridge, Hertford, Bedford, Stamford and Nottingham) facing the other, "Danish" burh.

Like his father Edward, King Athelstan (924-939) attempted to restrict all trade to market places in towns, burhs and ports, where trade could be properly witnessed and a royal reeve could collect tolls and taxes, the most important royal revenues. Kings needed cash, not cabbages, to maintain an army and build boats.

Buying and selling in the country – up on lande – were banned; this proved impractical and the law was relaxed. Nevertheless, the role of the old defended places as market centres was enhanced. Athelstan also confined all minting of coins to boroughs (in East Anglia at Norwich, later Ipswich and Thetford) and banned Sunday trading.

On extending West Saxon rule, Edward broke up Mercia, his rival kingdom, into small parts called shires, each of which was ruled from and named after its main town – hence Cambridgeshire, Warwickshire and Staffordshire. A reeve or sheriff was appointed to each shire. It is possible that at this time Norfolk and Suffolk were formally divided.

Edward imposed a new system of "hundreds," divisions of the shire, as the unit of taxation, justice and military service. The hundred eventually had its own court, held in the open at a prominent place such as a ford or barrow (hoe). Some hundreds, including Mitford, Freebridge, Grimshoe, Spelhoe and Forehoe, were named after these places.

Rough justice

Anglo-Saxons lived in a violent rural society in which many crimes went unseen. With no police, savage penalties were laid down to discourage offenders. Convicted criminals were bound and then hung, decapitated, strangled or throat-cut.

Responsibility for tracking down wrongdoers rested with groups of "tithing men," who were appointed to each hundred and raised the hue-and-cry. They pursued the criminal with a posse and faced punishment themselves if they failed to catch him – or if they caught the wrong man.

Anglo-Saxon justice was essentially a matter of vengeance, executed in the public eye at the hundred court. Cases were heard on the basis of oath against oath.

Much retribution was private and never reached courts. Bloodfeuds or vendettas between families were still so common that King Edmund (939-946) condemned them as unchristian and tried to ban them.

Edmund wanted the criminal to stand alone and take full responsibility for his actions without involving his family. His relations were urged to disown the wrongdoer and refuse to pay any compensation on his behalf.

The grim reality of formalised Anglo-Saxon justice, with its open-air courts and capital punishments, was revealed by the recent excavation of a macabre and remarkable site at South Acre, near Swaffham.

Close to the boundary of South Greenhoe hundred one of a group of prehistoric barrows was dug in 1987-88. It unexpectedly contained about 100 rough and shallow graves cut into the filling of the ditch around the barrow mound.

Into these graves the criminals' bodies had been carelessly dumped, their limbs askew and with skulls missing or placed between or beside legs. Some had probably been trussed up before execution.

The graves date to the 8th and 9th centuries and all the evidence points to them being on an execution site. Gallows may have stood high above the barrow.

The contemporary poem, The Fates of Men, says: "One must ride on the crooked gallows, hang to death until the living body, bloody dwelling of bone, becomes broken. There the raven takes an eye from him, the dark-coated creature tears the lifeless one ... His life is fled, and he senseless, without hope of life. Pale on the beam he endures his fate, covered with the mist of death. Sad is his name."

All criminals were held to be heathen and were denied the comforts of a Christian burial. Their bodies were cast into lonely graves in unconsecrated ground, often at crossroads or old boundaries, or at the place of execution.

String 'em up – Late Saxon 'justice' from a contemporary manuscript.

CHURCH AND STATE

A vice-regent: Athelstan Half-King and his family and the revival of the Church

The West Saxon kings rarely strayed beyond the borders of their ancestral kingdom of Wessex, relying instead on trusted ealdormen to run affairs in the rest of England. Ealdormen were virtually vice-regents who met the king in councils and at the great church festivals, such as Christmas and Easter.

In East Anglia, the remarkable family of ealdorman Athelstan (who gained the nickname Half-King) governed for much of the 10th century (from 932 to 992) and were at the very centre of the turbulent politics of court and church. Their power and prestige, enhanced by both Danish and English subordinates, kept the region loyal to the king and held off renewed Danish attacks until 991.

Athelstan's family were also at the heart of church revival. Reform was sorely needed: at the beginning of the 10th century church authority in eastern England was still shattered by Danish invasion and settlement. A Peterborough monk wrote that Ivar's Danes "destroyed all the monasteries they came to."

Those who settled were soon converted to Christianity but no attempt was made to refound the centres of ecclesiastical authority – the old monasteries, which were staffed by married clerks who shared out monastic land between them, and the bishopric. The seizure of monastic property by laymen was as heavy a blow to the church as the attacks by the Vikings.

Throughout East Anglia a growing trend developed for the establishment of "private" village churches. With few controls, new landowners aspired to build their own churches on their estates. It was a trend which deprived the old mother churches of income and influence.

King Edmund (939-946) sought to stamp out laxity in monasteries and protect the revenues of the mother churches by attempting to remove married clerks and denying a Christian burial to those who committed adultery or who had sexual intercourse with nuns (the wives of married clerks).

The seeds of reform were sown by three great churchmen – Dunstan, who became Archbishop of Canterbury, Oswald, Bishop of Worcester, and Aethelwold, Bishop of Winchester. All were monks, much influenced by monastic reforms on the continent, and they began a movement which

The Whissonsett cross, one of the very few surviving Late Saxon decorated ecclesiastical pieces of stonework in Norfolk.

revived the church on strict monastic lines.

They realised the need to gain the king's help and protection but had to wait for a willing ruler. Chief of their allies was Athelstan Half-King, a close friend also inspired by reform who had a special relationship with the future King Edgar the Peaceable (born 943), the son of King Edmund. When Edmund remarried he sent his small son away to Athelstan, who raised him as part of his own family (he had two sons, Ethelwold and Ethelwine).

Young Edgar grew up with Ethelwine before being sent away to be schooled by Aethelwold, a family friend who was then abbot of Abingdon. He thus spent his formative years completely within Athelstan's circle. He even married the widow of Ethelwold, his foster-brother.

After becoming king in 959 at the age of 16, Edgar took the lead in promoting church reform, encountering the fierce opposition of the clerks and laymen who had taken over monastic property. He also protected the mother churches against the growing threat of private "thegnly" churches.

A great plague in 962, seen as punishment for neglecting the church, was the spur for action. Rather reluctantly, Edgar decided to allow the thegn who built a church with its own graveyard (a private village church)

(a)   *(b)*

(a) From Magdalen Street, Norwich, a Late Saxon disc brooch with a backward-facing quadruped; a common decoration on small brooches of the period.

(b) Another common Late Saxon disc brooch type, from the Anglia TV site in Norwich, decorated with interlace in the Viking 'Borre' style (late 9th-early 10th century).

to divert some tithes to maintain a priest. But, for the first time, thegns and villagers were also held individually responsible for supporting the church with their dues.

Edgar's laws were also an attempt to protect the payment of tithes, church scot and plough alms to the mother churches. This was resented by many thegns and villagers who now had their own church to maintain.

In 964 Edgar turned to the monasteries and their married staff, ousting the secular clergy from ecclesiastical centres and refounding many of the destroyed monasteries. He staffed them with celibate monks whose allegiance was to their abbot and the rule of St Benedict rather than the landowners. Edgar's reforms were carried out with the encouragement of Aethelwold, Dunstan and Oswald, and Athelstan Half-King.

Athelstan and his son Ethelwine were instrumental in the refounding of the ancient monastic houses of Peterborough, Thorney and Ely and a great new house at Ramsey under the special patronage of Ethelwine, "Friend of God," who gave it much land and influence. For example, Ramsey was given all profits of justice in Clackclose hundred, money from Brancaster for clothing, food rent from Hickling and 60,000 eels from Wells.

The ancient foundation of Ely had decayed and was staffed by a few priests; many of Ely's lands had fallen into the hands of laymen who had leased them. Under Edgar, Bishop Aethelwold drove out the priests and recovered much for Ely, where a new cult of St Etheldreda was encouraged and a new church built to house the relics of St Etheldreda, her sister Sexburga and those of another sister, Withburga, purloined from West Dereham for this purpose, which symbolised divine protection of the new monastery and its property.

East Anglia did not benefit directly from the church revival until the reign of Cnut, which saw the refounding of Bury St Edmunds, a new church there for the remains of Edmund, and the creation of the Abbey of St Benet-at-Holme, near Horning, which may have been a monastic site in the pre-Danish period.

Into a northern empire

East Anglia enjoyed a period of peace lasting more than 60 years following Edward the Elder's reconquest of the region in 917. Tension between East Anglians and the English king relaxed and between 952 and 956 a new diocese based at North Elmham was established for Norfolk and Suffolk by King Eadred. Its first bishop was Eadwulf.

With peace came prosperity. Norwich and Thetford flourished and countryside settlements expanded far beyond their 9th century limits. At Thetford, for example, the great town ditch and rampart were levelled and covered by urban sprawl.

The relative freedoms retained by the region's Anglo-Danish population helped stimulate much of the economic dynamism of the period. The Danish liberties recognised in the legislation of King Edgar the Peaceable (959-975) contrasted with the status of Englishmen, who were subject to the king's laws.

Edgar's tolerance was not universally admired. One commentator wrote of him: "He loved evil foreign customs and brought too firmly heathen manners within the land, and attracted hither foreigners and enticed harmful people to this country."

Ethelred II, later known as the Unready, ascended the throne as a boy in 978 to a background of dynastic rivalry and murder which set much of his kingdom against his rule. He inherited a country on the verge of civil war.

Within two years Viking raids were again causing havoc along the coasts of England, possibly because the Danish King Harold had set about the conversion of his realm to Christianity, producing exiles who, wishing to remain pagan, left Scandinavia to seek their fortunes in England, which was by then disunited and distracted.

A massive Viking army ravaged Ipswich in 991, prompting a battle at Maldon in Essex, made famous by a great Anglo-Saxon poem. Despite the noble courage of the English, who were led by their ealdorman, the Vikings achieved an important victory which led to a treaty giving the invaders the immense sum of 22,000 pounds of gold and silver.

The fortune was raised through taxation, and similar attempts to buy off the Vikings seriously weakened the English economy over the remainder of

Ethelred's long reign. The levying of the tax, later known as Danegeld, only encouraged further and larger invasions.

In a desperate bid to regain control of his kingdom, Ethelred ordered the massacre of Danes in England on St Brice's Day (November 13) 1002. The order cannot have been carried out in Danish areas such as East Anglia but, by awful chance, one victim was Gunnhild, sister of the powerful King Swein of Denmark.

The next year Swein invaded the south west of England with a huge force and in 1004 he sailed to East Anglia and sacked Norwich. It was an attack in which "corselets ran red in Norwich," a Danish poem later recalled.

While local leaders sued for peace, Swein's army then turned its destructive attention to Thetford. Ulfketel Snilling, an Anglo-Danish leader and possibly an ealdorman, led a force to confront the invaders near Thetford but the Danes won the day, despite sustaining heavy losses. They then left the country, their withdrawal made possible by the failure of the East Anglians to destroy the Danes' ships following an order to do so from Ulfketel.

Swein again pounced on England in 1009. Ipswich was taken in the spring of 1010, and soon after the East Anglians were defeated at Ringmere (either Ringmere in Wretham parish, four miles north east of Thetford, or Rymer, four miles to the south). The East Anglians, assisted by the men of Cambridgeshire, were defeated after a fierce struggle.

In 1012 the Danes withdrew after murdering the Archbishop of Canterbury only to return with Swein, who was intent on becoming king of the English. The old Danelaw rapidly accepted him as king.

The unfortunate King Ethelred, who also faced internal revolt, fled the country at the end of 1013 but Swein died almost immediately afterwards. His second son, Cnut, invaded in 1015 and, following a decisive victory at Ashingdon in Essex, was soon in a position to divide England between himself and Ethelred's son and successor, Edmund Ironside, who was left with the old kingdom of Wessex.

Within months Edmund too died and Cnut, the king of Denmark, became king of all England. He was accepted swiftly by a country tired of war and internal strife. In 1028 Cnut took the crown of Norway.

The people of Norfolk, for so long a mixture of Anglo-Saxon and Dane, thus became subjects of a northern empire which held sway on both sides of the North Sea.

Late Saxon society

The 10th and 11th centuries were times of great social upheaval in East Anglia. With the spread of prosperity and personal freedoms many

A late Saxon lead brooch from Oxborough. The legend of the design crudely copies contemporary coins.

newly-prosperous Saxons claimed social rank not theirs by birth.

In an effort to protect the privileges and rights of the "old nobility," new laws were introduced to define the rights and obligations of each stratum of society. The laws specified, for example, that in order for a ceorl to become a thegn, or estate owner, he had to possess a church, a seat in the king's hall and, most important of all, five hides of land (about 600 acres).

A long, rambling contemporary tract called the Rights and Ranks of People detailed the duties of the thegn and the three classes beneath him, the geneat, cottar and boor.

The thegn's duties were "public" services to the monarch. He had to provide men for armed service, repair burhs and bridges and the king's fences, and help equip the fleet. The geneat had duties to his lord. In addition to paying rent in cash he had to ride and carry for his lord and repair his hall. The cottar paid no rent but provided labour services on the lord's demesne at specified times in the week and at harvest time. He was given land (normally five acres), tools and utensils, but all had to be returned to his lord at death.

The boor, lower down the social scale, provided labour services and paid rent in barley, hens, sheep and other animals from his own flocks. He was also expected to have a horse available to fulfil his duties. In earlier centuries the possession of a horse was a symbol of social status. The fact that by the 10th and 11th centuries lowly boors had use of them illustrates the extent to which Anglo-Saxon society had increased in wealth.

According to the tract, each estate worker had appropriate allowances and rights, from the hayward (who looked after meadows) to the woodward (woodman), the swineherd and the cowherd. The oxherd received shoes and gloves to do his work. The beekeeper had to pay honey as rent and cut corn and mow meadows.

The personal and intimate side of late Anglo-Saxon society is rarely glimpsed, but in one surviving document, the Betrothal of a Woman, advice is given on "how a man shall betroth a maiden." It shows that contemporary women were not expected to accept their suitors unwillingly.

The groom's friends acted as sureties for his promise that he would maintain the bride. This is how the convention of the best man as the "groom's guarantor" arose. All the kinsmen of both bride and groom witnessed the marriage and agreed to its arrangements.

The groom had to pay the family of the bride for raising her, and there was an agreed sum as a morning gift to the bride. Only at the end of the document is the need for a priest mentioned.

The work of an ideal estate is brought to life in a tract called the Sagacious Reeve. The estate bailiff, or reeve, had, says the document, to "know the lord's landright, and the folkrights ... and the season of every crop." He had to be not "too lax or too overweening."

It goes on: "Let him pay attention to things great and small, so that neither go wrong ... neither corn nor sheaf ... nor flesh nor cream ... nor cheese nor rennet." It ends with a long list of all the equipment the reeve had to have, including tools for all trades, kitchen equipment and even a mousetrap.

Not all was upward mobility in the late Anglo-Saxon period. Countless numbers of people were reduced to servitude, forced into selling themselves and their families in return for food and protection from famine, the reversion of estates to monasteries, war and general life-chances. Ethelred even had to legislate that no Christian could be sold abroad into slavery.

There were few ways out of servitude unless a pious lord, perhaps a churchman, released his slaves in his will, giving them freedom in an act of manumission – "for the love of God, and for the need of his soul."

For example, when Ketel the thegn was about to go to Rome on pilgrimage in the 1050s he made his will, granting his estate at Harling, near Thetford, to the church, "just as it stands, except that the men shall be free." Otherwise, slaves were closely bound to their lord and his demesne farm, the heavy routine of the farming calendar and the rule of the reeve. The thegn was still a warrior; Ketel bequeathed to his lord, Archbishop Stigand, his heriot – a helmet, a coat of mail, a horse with harness and a sword and a spear.

The village church

By the later 10th century many Norfolk villages had a church – so many, in fact, that the laws of Edmund and Edgar made it a duty for both lords and villagers to maintain "their" church with tithes and taxes.

The village churches may have been of stone, but this was unusual; they were more often of wood, like the two churches excavated at Norwich and Thetford, which would have resembled little more than peasants' houses. Inside, they were plastered and brightly painted with pictures of saints, Bethlehem and, as a grim warning to all, the Last Judgement.

The churches may have been hung with embroideries, and their priests, employed by the lord and perhaps a member of his family, would have said Mass in Latin, resplendent in silk robes and officiating with a silver dish and cup. At services they read from lavishly ornamented gospel books. To the people, the church was a door to another world. The church calendar measured the course of the seasons, with their feasts and fasts, weekly routines and days of rest. Much attention was focused on the "holy days" and, above all, the patronal feast when the saint of the parish church would be honoured and much ale and food consumed. The church calendar held the chief rent-paying times of Easter and Michaelmas.

Hardship and famine were ever-present worries and the church, with its promise of heavenly reward, literally understood, made the harsh world easier to bear.

King Cnut and the origins of the 1066 invasion

As king of England, Denmark and Norway, King Cnut had to rule three kingdoms, often at a distance. To consolidate his power he dismissed or executed English leaders and ealdormen whom he distrusted and replaced them with "earls" in four newly-created earldoms.

The Chronicle says in 1017: "In this year King Cnut divided (England) into four parts ... giving East Anglia to Thurkil the Tall."

Chief among the earls was Godwin, earl of Wessex, who was loyal to Cnut (to whom he was related by marriage). Eventually his sons became earls also, and one of them, Harold Godwinson, grew to seek more and more power until even the crown itself seemed within reach.

A ruthless yet pious man, Cnut made efforts to support the English church, refounding St Benet-at-Holme and founding a regular monastery at Bury St Edmunds "to look after the body of the saint."

In an effort to win over his new English subjects he set aside his first wife, a Mercian girl called Elgifu (who had borne him two sons, Harold Harefoot and Swein), in favour of Queen Emma, King Ethelred's widow.

Though it helped secure his English crown, Cnut's marriage to Emma complicated the question of the succession as it brought together the English, Norman and Danish royal houses. As the daughter of Duke

Richard I of Normandy, Emma introduced a potential Norman claim to the throne.

Throughout her marriages to Ethelred and Cnut until her own death in 1052 she was at the heart of claims to the crown which ended in the double invasion of 1066.

Ethelred and Emma had had two sons, Alfred and Edward. On her remarriage to Cnut she put them out of harm's way by exiling both to Normandy. She and Cnut had a son, Harthacnut.

Cnut's death in 1035 left the crown poised between various claimants, backed by rival interests in the old kingdoms. Mercian interests naturally preferred Harold Harefoot, elder son of Elgifu, Cnut's Mercian ex-wife. But Emma and Godwin supported Harthacnut.

Emma's elder son, Alfred, returned from exile in 1036 to restore the Anglo-Norman dynasty but tradition tells us that he was trapped and brutally killed by the Godwins.

Harold Harefoot emerged out of the chaos to take the throne in 1037 but lived only three years. The crown then passed to the sickly Harthacnut who died, unmarried and childless, in 1042, still a young man.

Harthacnut had recognised the claim of his half brother Edward and in the same year he returned from exile in France to restore the Anglo-Norman line. By now a middle-aged and childless bachelor, Edward was a stranger to England and fell under the dominating influence of the all-powerful Godwins. He married Earl Godwin's daughter, Edith, and his new in-laws came to virtually rule all England.

Conflict was inevitable as Edward's childless reign drew to a close, with three powerful men poised to claim the throne. When Edward died in 1066 one of them, Harold Godwinson, a son of the old earl of Wessex, seized the crown for himself, "before the funeral meats were barely cold."

The other two claimants, the great warriors Harold Hardrada of Norway and Duke William of Normandy, made immediate preparations to invade Harold's kingdom. Hardrada attacked Yorkshire with a fleet of 300 ships but was defeated by Harold in the great battle of Stamford Bridge. All but 24 ships were destroyed.

The beleaguered Harold then heard of William's arrival in Sussex and marched his exhausted troops to the south. "At the hoary apple tree" of Hastings they were defeated in October, 1066. Harold lost his life and the crown of England. Duke William became king of England.

Securing the Norman kingdom

The Battle of Hastings was the beginning of William's conquest, not the end. He faced great resistance for many years, particularly from the north.

He had invaded England with the help of powerful Norman barons who naturally sought reward for their support. This came in the form of land which was seized from the English and distributed among the allies.

Of the 10,000 men who crossed the channel some 2000 were rewarded with gifts of land. Before long, 10 of William's relatives and favourites owned 30 per cent of England's land. Among them were two major Norfolk landowners, the Bigod and Warenne families. Much of the rest of England was held by William and the Norman church.

English landowners all but disappeared, replaced by the king's men. Around the time of the conquest Edwin, a Norfolk thegn and large landowner, made a will bequeathing gifts to the church at St Benet's and Bury. It took no effect as his estates were lost to a Norman, Godric the Dapifer.

The man appointed by William to hold down East Anglia, Earl Ralph the Gael, a Breton, was one of William's less reliable allies. He held Norwich Castle for the crown but led East Anglia into a brief revolt in 1075 which was promptly suppressed by the king's close friend, William de Warenne. Ralph fled to Britanny and his earldom went to Roger Bigod, a trusted ally.

The East Anglian See

Struggling to gain control of England, William appointed his favourites to bishoprics as well as earldoms.

One of two intrically carved pieces of 11th century stonework at the Grammar School, Thetford; perhaps once part of the short-lived cathedral there.

As soon as the king's appointments started to sweep the land, Althelmaer's days as Bishop of East Anglia were numbered. Born of Anglo-Scandinavian stock, he had been at Elmham since 1052 and was the brother of Stigand. His bishopric was poor and his cathedral was said to be little more than a simple church of wood and daub.

By the decree of Archbishop Lanfranc, Althelmaer was deposed in 1070 and Herfast, a Norman royal favourite, put in his place under instructions to find a more suitable site for his bishopric.

Believing the English church to be slack and backward, the Normans followed continental practice in putting their bishops in towns rather than in out-of-the-way villages such as Elmham. The only East Anglian towns of consequence were Norwich, Thetford, Ipswich and Bury St Edmunds, which was already the home of a wealthy abbey. Herfast chose to move from Elmham to Thetford, making the church of St Mary the Greater – now the site of Thetford Grammar School – his cathedral.

Herfast's ambition was to take over the abbey at Bury St Edmunds but this was thwarted by its formidable abbot, Baldwin, a Frenchman who had been appointed by Edward the Confessor in 1065. Baldwin fought to keep his abbey independent, waging a dogged campaign which won the eventual support of the king and even the Pope.

By the time of the Domesday Book (1086), the abbot had knocked down the old Saxon settlement of Bury and laid out a "new town," with a distinctive grid street pattern and vast market place to serve the abbey and the "body of the saint." In 1095, two years before Baldwin died, Edmund's relics were installed in a large new stone church in the town.

Meanwhile, the East Anglian see was on the move yet again. By the time Bishop Herbert de Losinga was appointed in 1091 it was already planned to move it from Thetford to Norwich where, according to the Domesday Book, William had given houses "for the seat of the bishopric" and granted permission for the establishment of a mint for the bishop. A huge cathedral began to rise in Norwich in the 1090s.

The scale of the cathedral overwhelmed any Saxon church. Two earlier churches had to be demolished to make way for it. It was monastic, with room for 60 monks, and set in its own precincts within the Saxon town. The bishop's palace was built in the style of a keep, possibly for defensive reasons.

Meanwhile, throughout Norfolk, the wood and thatch churches of the Anglo-Saxons gave way to the new Norman architecture of stone.

The English language, brought in by the Angles and Saxons centuries earlier, was eclipsed by French, which became the tongue of the royal circle, the church, the aristocracy and the law courts.

Anglo-Saxons followed their new masters, patronising the new Norman churches and abbeys and adopting French and French names, such as William, Hubert, Ralph and Richard.

Norwich

Norwich changed dramatically after the conquest. Local children of 1066 must have grown up to marvel at the energy of their Norman masters, who wasted no time in building the castle, cathedral and the "French borough," with its great market place, which still exists.

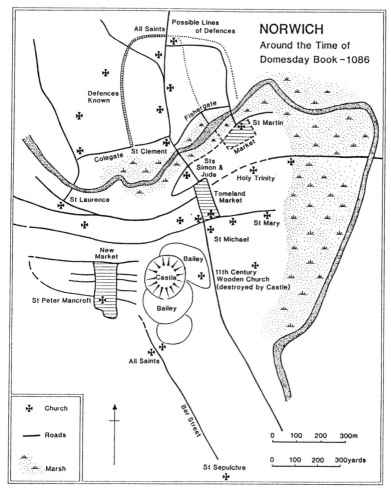

Norwich around 1086, showing the main elements of the Anglo-Saxon town and the new Norman features, the castle, and the New Market. The bishop moved to Norwich and began his new cathedral near Holy Trinity in 1094.

When they arrived in Norwich, William's men found what was already one of the largest and most important Saxon towns in England. It had 1320 burgesses, or freemen (mostly merchants and traders), indicating a total population of between 5000-10,000, and many churches.

Mention is made in the Domesday Book of All Saints (possibly in All Saints' Green or Magdalen Street), St Martin-at-Palace, St Michael (Tombland), Holy Trinity, SS Simon and Jude (near Fye Bridge) and one held by the abbot of Bury, St Laurence (Westwick Street). All are thought to have been Saxon.

For centuries, Norwich had been a busy port. Its waterfront lay on the stretch of the Wensum between the Whitefriars and Fye bridges, where shallow draft boats could be drawn up on gently shelving beaches, tied to simple wooden jetties and unloaded.

"Strand" streets, now represented by the curving lines of Fishergate, ran parallel to the river jetties. Rude huts along the streets provided warehousing. Another street to the south of the river has been lost over time but its route can be seen from ancient property boundaries. A market place (Palace Plain), where traders and merchants haggled over goods and animals, ran along the side of the southern street, possibly with its own church, St Martin-at-Palace.

The main pre-conquest market place, however, was Tombland (meaning empty place), a large rectangular area with the richest church in town, St Michael (subsequently destroyed). Industry sold its products on the stalls of Tombland, including pots from nearby Pottergate, where many pottery kilns have been discovered.

After 1066, Norwich's new overlords swept aside 98 houses and a church to make way for the building of the wooden castle (later rebuilt in stone) and its bailey to provide the Normans with a defensive highpoint overlooking the Saxon town. It was completed by 1070.

By 1086, the Normans had laid out plans for a typical "French borough," with a single dominating church – St Peter Mancroft – and a great market place beside it. A few years later, Herbert de Losinga's cathedral was begun in the heart of the old Saxon town.

Thetford

Thetford was a town of the first rank with a population of between 4000 and 5000 at the time of the conquest. It had a monastery, a mint rendering £40 to the king and (soon after 1066) a castle later held by Earl Roger Bigod.

In common with other ancient and important Saxon towns it was a place of many churches. Twelve are mentioned in the Domesday Book, including St Peter, St John, St Martin, St Margaret and the minster church of St Mary, which was then still the cathedral of East Anglia.

Like Norwich and Ipswich, Thetford had suffered the ravages of the Danes but its economic expansion was maintained. By the late 10th century the settlement had spilled over its earlier defences south of the river.

Thetford's growth was reversed by the conquest. In 1066 it had 943 burgesses. Twenty years later there were 720.

Yarmouth and Lynn

The Domesday Book says little about Yarmouth, a small borough on a long sand spit at the Yare-mouth, served by its own church, St Benet's, the site of which is unknown.

Yarmouth was held by the king, and his 70 burgesses paid him eighteen pounds for their freedoms. No mention is made of Yarmouth's fishermen, even though 24 are recorded across the water at Gorleston. Under the instructions of Bishop de Losinga a new town was subsequently built with a vast market place dominated by the newly-erected priory church of St Nicholas, a cell to Norwich.

At the other end of his ecclesiastical empire the Norman bishop set about laying out another new town at Lynn (meaning pool), with the great church of St Margaret, built on the "sand market" on the foreshore where trade was already taking place. The church dominates the Saturday Market Place, where the bishop granted a market. He also gave permission for a fair to be held on the feast of St Margaret, the patron saint.

Maltings and swine, meadows and mills

For all its detail, the Domesday Book presents a confusing image of rural Norfolk at the end of the Saxon period. William's diligent commissioners gathered such a mass of information from landlords and tenants that it is sometimes difficult to discern a general picture of contemporary life.

Nonetheless, the Domesday Book reveals a populous landscape of more than 700 Norfolk villages. Some coastal settlements, including Shipden and Snitterly, were already in the process of being washed away by the sea.

However, we can see that by the time of the conquest many of Norfolk's smaller land holdings – minor hamlets, ancient assarts (that is, new settlements cut out of woods and waste) and farmsteads – had separated from parent villages and were by then counted as independent settlements.

They included the -thorps, -thwaites, -worths and -steads (Bagthorpe, Gaytonthorpe, Themelthorpe, Thwaite, Spixworth, Ranworth, Tunstead and Worstead). Another example, Guestwick, recorded in the Domesday Book as Guistthwaite, had once been an area of pasture for the people of Guist. But by the 11th century it was an independent settlement with its own church.

Over the rest of Britain land was usually divided into manors, with lords holding demesne and tenants having land and stock in return for services and rent to the lord. With its great number of freemen and rent-paying peasants living alongside lords and their tenants, Norfolk was different.

The amount of land held by Norfolk's freemen varied greatly. Some scratched a living from plots of only a few acres. At Gissing, eight freemen held 60 acres, while at Dickleburgh, four held 20 acres. In his will of about 1038, freeman Thurketel of Palgrave left 20 acres to be shared between four heirs.

Freemen were liable to pay taxes but they could buy and sell their land freely, a privilege denied to the majority of Anglo-Saxons. Minor tenants and peasants, none of whom are named in the Domesday Book, had few freedoms and owed rent and services to the lord and his demesne.

More and more of the Norfolk landscape was being turned over to arable farming to feed a growing population. The Domesday Book records some 5000 plough teams county-wide. As the cultivated landscape expanded so remaining woodland became increasingly precious, particularly in central-south Norfolk.

The king's commissioners measured woods carefully, and even small patches were described as woodlands for so many swine. At Hevingham, for example, there was "wood for 18 swine and two-thirds of another." At Hempnall there was "wood for 200 swine." At Costessey, mention is also made of a deer park.

In East Anglia, where lordship was relatively weak and freedoms more widespread, the ungoverned running of freemen's stock may have contributed to the decline of common wood pastures, turning them into the open heath commons of the middle ages.

Rivers, meadows and fisheries were recorded by the commissioners in meticulous detail. Rivers were enormously important to the economy of late Saxon Norfolk and along them stood approximately 300 corn-grinding watermills. In addition, 61 river fisheries were noted across the county, besides that at Yarmouth. The Church held Friday to be a meatless day (though poverty made most days meatless for many) and fish were an important part of contemporary diets.

Fish and other meats could only be preserved through summer and winter with salt, which came from salterns in the Yare valley and West Norfolk and the Fens, often held by monastic houses and "upland" manors.

The village church was by then commonplace; the Domesday Book mentions 217 in Norfolk, far fewer than actually existed. No church is mentioned at Colkirk, for example, despite the fact that its name (kirk) means church, or at other places where we know a church stood. Other examples include East Dereham, Pulham, Feltwell, Northwold, Walton and Terrington.

Many of the county's churches had been built privately by thegns near their manor houses or by groups of freemen. And churches were popular – Edwin left bequests to 12 churches in East Anglia. Sometimes we hear of the priests; a priest at Hevingham with 40 acres and another at Witton with 30 acres had each to sing three masses for their land.

In the Fens, settlement was still confined to a string of villages on higher ground on the seaward rim of the great Fen basin, and villagers ran vast flocks of sheep over the lush grassland of nearby Marshland. Walton had two flocks, of 800 and 1300 sheep. All this the commissioners saw and counted.

Conclusion

The Norfolk landscape contains so few visible remains of its Anglo-Saxon past that we might be excused the assumption that the period between the 5th and 11th centuries was of little import in the development of our society.

It is not, however, in the buildings, earthworks and field systems of the county that we can see the Anglo-Saxons' mark, but in the place names, the English language and legal system.

The Bronze Age peoples of the second millenium before Christ studded the poorer soils of the county with numerous mounds which survive today, and the Romans left us the mighty walls of Burgh Castle and Caistor St Edmund. But we are indebted to our Anglo-Saxon ancestors whenever we speak, follow a signpost or attend a law court.

The study of Anglo-Saxon history and archaeology is still flourishing, and in the years ahead many of the outstanding gaps in our knowledge will, it is hoped, be filled. This will involve the reinterpretation of information available currently, particularly in documentary sources, and most especially in the vast body of data contained in the Domesday Book.

Place name research has also a long way to go. As yet, no county-wide study of place names has been published. It is in archaeology that there rests the greatest opportunity to learn more about the period. With the present state of funding, the towns, Norwich, Thetford and Yarmouth, will benefit the most from archaeological excavation, and in future we should learn a great deal about the Anglo-Saxon origins of these places.

The countryside has only just started to yield up its secrets. A steady stream of information now flows into the county archaeological archives at Norwich Castle Museum and Gressenhall. This information consists, in the main, of surface finds of pottery and metalwork made by archaeologists both amateur and professional as well as metal detector users. The settlement history of a few individual villages and parishes is now reasonably well understood, and the discoveries of hitherto unknown cemetery sites are now reported regularly.

As sites are recorded, and their locations plotted, the aim of understanding social systems, settlement dynamics and land use over the 600 years of Anglo-Saxon Norfolk will become possible. All this fieldwork will, it is hoped, be supplemented by the excavation of settlements, cemeteries and churches.

In this way, our knowledge of particular sites can be applied to the vast majority that will remain unexcavated and known only from surface finds. If all goes well in historical, archaeological and place name research in the years ahead, a new edition of this book will be needed, perhaps before the start of the new millenium.

Anglo-Saxon pottery site showing cut-away of kiln with pots.

Warning

Reference to or representation of a site should not be taken as evidence that such a site may be visited. In almost every case sites are on private land. If permission to view is obtained it is of the utmost importance that sites, and crops and soils covering or surrounding them, should not be disturbed in any way.

Places to visit

Norwich Castle Museum, Castle Meadow, Norwich (Norwich 222222)
Yarmouth Museum, 4 South Quay, Great Yarmouth
(Great Yarmouth 855746)
King's Lynn Museum, Old Market Street, King's Lynn
(King's Lynn 775001)
Thetford Ancient House Museum, White Hart Street, Thetford
(Thetford 752599)
Cromer Museum, East Cottages, Tucker Street, Cromer
(Cromer 513543)

Metal detectors

Found objects, other than those of gold and silver, belong to the landowner and not to the tenant or finder. Gold and silver objects are subject to a Treasure Trove inquest and must be reported to the local Coroner, though this can be done for you by the local museum. It is important to remember that all land belongs to someone, and prior permission to use a metal detector is thus required. Metal detector users are encouraged to report their finds to the Norfolk Museums Service so that objects of interest can be recorded. Sensible use of metal detectors is to be welcomed; and a pamphlet ("Archaeological Finds: Some Suggestions about the Use of Metal Detectors in Norfolk and Suffolk") has been compiled by the Scole Archaeological Committee. Copies are available from the Norfolk Archaeological Unit, Union House, Gressenhall, East Dereham, Norfolk NR20 4DR. In addition a number of special clubs for detector users have been formed. Ask at the Unit for details.

Organisations to join

Norfolk and Norwich Archaeological Society, Garsett House, St Andrews Hall Plain, Norwich NR3 1AT

Great Yarmouth and District Archaeological Society, c/o Central Library, Great Yarmouth

West Norfolk and King's Lynn Archaeological Society, c/o King's Lynn Museum, King's Lynn

Norfolk Industrial Archaeology Society, c/o The Bridewell Museum, Norwich

Norfolk Archaeological Rescue Group, c/o Norfolk Archaeological Unit, Union House, Gressenhall, East Dereham, Norfolk NR20 4DR

Norfolk Research Committee, c/o 13 Heigham Grove, Norwich

(A list of other societies is usually available from the Information Service, Norwich Central Library, Bethel Street, Norwich)

Index

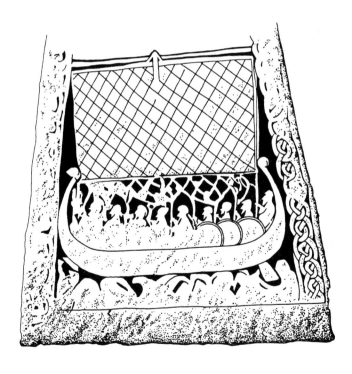